MODERNIST WOMEN WRITERS AND WAR

MODERNIST WOMEN WRITERS AND WAR

Trauma and the Female Body in Djuna Barnes, H.D., and Gertrude Stein

Julie Goodspeed-Chadwick

LOUISIANA STATE UNIVERSITY PRESS
BATON ROUGE

Published by Louisiana State University Press

Manufactured in the United States of America
First printing

DESIGNER: Mandy McDonald Scallan
TYPEFACES: Text, Whitman; Display, Mrs.Eaves
PRINTER: McNaughton & Gunn, Inc.
BINDER: Dekker and Sons, Inc.

Library of Congress Cataloging-in-Publication Data

Goodspeed-Chadwick, Julie, 1978–
Modernist women writers and war : trauma and the female body in Djuna Barnes, H.D., and Gertrude Stein / Julie Goodspeed-Chadwick.
p. cm.
Includes bibliographical references and index.
ISBN 978-0-8071-3681-2 (cloth : alk. paper) 1. American literature—Women authors—History and criticism. 2. World War, 1939–1945—Literature and the war. 3. Barnes, Djuna. 4. H. D. (Hilda Doolittle), 1886–1961. 5. Stein, Gertrude, 1874–1946. 6. Women and war in literature. 7. Psychic trauma in literature. 8. Modernism (Literature)—United States. 9. Women and literature—United States—History—20th century. I. Title.

PS151.G58 2010
810.9'352209044—dc22

2010009338

The paper in this book meets the guidelines for permanence and durability of the Committee on Production Guidelines for Book Longevity of the Council on Library Resources. ∞

This book is dedicated
to my mother,
Barb Goodspeed (1952–2005);
to my brother,
Terry Goodspeed;
and to my husband,
Keith Chadwick.

— Contents —

— *Acknowledgments* —

The first readers of this manuscript deserve special acknowledgment: Deborah M. Mix, Ball State University; Kristie S. Fleckenstein, Florida State University; Patrick C. Collier, Ball State University; Rai Peterson, Ball State University; and David Concepcion, Ball State University. I am indebted to them for their dedication in reviewing this project and for their exemplary professionalism and good humor. In short they are astute scholars, engaging teachers, and professional role models.

The readers affiliated with Louisiana State University Press also deserve special recognition. I was asked to reconsider this project in various ways, and this book exists in its current state as a result of the suggestions I received and implemented.

This study would not exist without the librarians at Ball State University and at Indiana University–Purdue University at Columbus (IUPUC), who bore the brunt of my countless requests for books and articles. Their work in locating and securing materials for me deserves greater praise than I can offer here. In particular Christina Kelley of the University Library of Columbus has been indispensable to my research.

I would also like to thank my friends at Indiana University–Purdue University at Columbus, as well as my former colleagues at Nicholls State University in Louisiana, for their collegiality and congeniality.

Additionally, I would like to recognize the impact that my students have had on me, notably in prompting me to think about the importance of what we do as scholars and teachers. In particular the students in my Studies in Women and Literature and Feminist Theory classes (fall 2007 at Nicholls and spring 2009 at IUPUC) and the students in my Literary Theory course (spring 2008 at Nicholls) continue to remind me of the significance of English studies and what is at stake in scholarship on literature and critical theory in academia and in the world outside of the book.

My methodology has also been influenced and bolstered by a host of scholars and teachers at Ball State and at Marian University, Indianapolis. I have had the great fortune to study and work with truly inspiring people.

It is with gratitude that I express my appreciation for John W. Easterly, Executive Editor at Louisiana State University Press, who embodies the ideal scholarly editor. Elizabeth Gratch deserves special acknowledgment for her careful and insightful reading of this manuscript and for her expert copyediting suggestions. At LSU Press, Lee C. Sioles navigated this book through the final stages to production with grace and adroitness. I must also thank Kristi Whitfield for suggesting that I send this project to LSU Press, and I thank the various people at the press who made this book what it is.

Lastly, I wish to leave my closing words to my family and close friends. Simply put, I am privileged to know them. They are the people who brighten my world each day and who offer the love and support that make this kind of endeavor possible.

MODERNIST WOMEN WRITERS AND WAR

Introduction

War Narratives

The authors in this study offer a different and much needed perspective on war: an embodied, feminist critique of trauma and the identity politics of war and war narratives. Rather than the traditional accounts of war by soldiers and male civilians depicting men in battle, the selected female authors investigate and engage with the gender politics of war and gendered writing and thereby contribute female civilian points of view. I argue for the critical consideration and validation of war writing by women, writing that does not always treat battles and refuses to foreground masculine attitudes toward war and women. Rather, Djuna Barnes, H.D., and Gertrude Stein counter patriarchal or traditional war narratives by featuring women as significant characters who suffer from war and protest it in their literary works. These writers create new narratives that cast war as destructive, perverse, traumatic, and quotidian. By recognizing women writers who write about marginalized aspects of war experience—namely, the experience of living on the home front economy in wartime, as war writers—we can likewise recognize a broader perspective on war experience and work toward a more accurate definition of war writing, one that takes into account women's responses to war and women's suffering.

The works of Barnes, H.D., and Stein participate in a genealogy of modernist female war writing that takes ownership of war as a subject for women writers. Although each writer takes a different approach in representing female bodies and experiences in connection with war, the order of the chapters highlights the progressively feminist and personal ownership of war embedded in the works by the selected authors. Barnes plays with conventional binary constructions in *Nightwood* (1936) to foster space for acknowledgment and validation of alterity; she suggestively places feminized bodies and feminized inanimate objects and animals in the vicinity of war to deplore the effects of war on women. H.D. invokes images of war trauma on the home front in *Trilogy* (1944–46), but she envisions a literary and spiritual template that encourages validation and inclusive healing from trauma. And Stein captures and documents her version of the daily reality of war in *Mrs. Reynolds* (1952) and her other war writings. Stein's emphasis on the quotidian nature of war positions it firmly within the domestic economy of Stein's household and her civilian purview. The repertoire of strategies employed by Barnes, H.D., and Stein engenders a new kind of literature: works that center female identity and validate female authorship of war narrative.

I use *narrative* in the sense of a master story, a fiction that teaches or reveals to us "the nature of things as they are" and allows us "to experiment with possible selves and to learn to take our places in the real world, to play our parts there" (Miller 69). I draw on J. Hillis Miller's discussion of narrative for my definition. He explains that narratives can be understood as revealing (the narrative shows us "the nature of things as they are" and thus provides a "place in which the reigning assumptions of a culture can be criticized") or creating meanings and ways of being in the world. From my perspective I think narratives both reveal and create at the same time. I do think "we need stories to make sense of our experience," but I also suspect that "we need the same stories over and over to reinforce that sense making" (70). Miller suggests that narrative, then, is "perhaps *the* most powerful" way "to assert the basic ideology of our culture." There is not, however, an end to the number of stories or narratives we can tell because no narrative can perfectly capture or relieve various ideological tensions or fulfill perfectly "its functions of ordering and confirming" (72). The literature I discuss in this study is crucial to changing our assumptions about war, gender, and American modernist women writers because their stories do not figure into the master narratives that are told and retold in the form of World War I and World War II canonical literature. I will discuss narrative in connection with poetry and novels because narratives perform cultural work by teaching lessons and building a "significant and orderly world" across genres (69).

What I refer to as "patriarchal war narrative" throughout the body of this study is what has traditionally been recognized as war poetry or war novels by outmoded and conservative categorical distinctions, consigning the subject of war to the province of men and male authors. The problem is not what has been counted as "war writing" but, rather, what has not been recognized as such. War writing for most of the twentieth century was thought to be war writing by men about men. Slowly, the genre of war writing has been expanded to include representations of war by female authors as scholars such as Margaret Higonnet agitate for recovery of female war writers and new ways of thinking about women, war, and literature: "The sustained bias of literary history against women who did write about war invites us to reexamine the stereotypical identification of women with propaganda and cliché. . . . Women's wartime involvements and depictions of war have been erased again and again from popular memory" (221). Although women's war writing is included with increasing frequency in twenty-first-century anthologies, there is still much work to be done in recovering female war writing and setting up critical frameworks within which to discuss women's literary depictions and treatments of war. Writing that has been classed as war writing can be written by civilians, but such writing is usually or predominantly gendered as male. I agree with Higonnet that an "important task has been to recognize the deficiency of a narrow definition of 'war' literature as 'authentic' autobiography produced by and about the trenches. . . . In order to recognize the fullness of women's contribution to this genre, we must reconceptualize war—and therefore the vocabulary of war—itself" (208). In order to grasp the bigger picture (one that includes women) and comprehend the "vocabulary," or the words of a language that characterize war more accurately, it is necessary to reconceptualize what war literature is and who writes it. In this study I focus on American modernist women writers, and I introduce female civilian authors as legitimate war writers who presented alternative perspectives on thinking and writing about war by critiquing it, engaging with identity politics, and deconstructing binary oppositions. Modernist women writers were certainly writing about war: Djuna Barnes alluded to war in her masterpiece novel *Nightwood* and in the notes toward her unfinished memoir; H.D. treated both World War I and World War II in her literary output; and Stein returned to war as her primary subject in various genres over a span of twenty years.

Yet it is poems such as W. B. Yeats's "An Irish Airman Foresees His Death" (1919) that are categorized as war narrative. "An Irish Airman" relies on a male perspective of war (a pilot contemplating the significance of his flight, his war duty, and his life while engaged in battle) and a male treatment of war (a male author imagining war situations). Predating Yeats's work is Amy Lowell's war poetry. Lowell attempts to capture the thoughts and experiences of soldiers in "The Allies" (1916), and this poem is not unlike Yeats's. Women have produced artistic treatments of war, but they have been prevented from claiming war as a legitimate subject; historically, women's literature on war has not been recognized as significant or meaningful. The binary oppositions that underpin and structure war as male activity and male experience distance women from war and prevent female writers from claiming war as their subject. Perhaps female authors have not claimed war in the same way as those (male) authors who are traditionally recognized as "war writers" have. But they do touch on "what gets left out . . . the emotional, the concrete, the particular, the human bodies and their vulnerability, human lives and their subjectivity—all of which are marked as feminine in the binary dichotomies of gender discourse" (Cohn 232). The authors I selected for this study initiate feminine and feminist strategies in their treatment of war that figure the home front economy and women's bodies in their texts in ways that are very different from those of their canonical male counterparts included in traditional anthologies. As a result, the war writings of Barnes, H.D., and Stein function as interventions into both literary and social history.

The strategies employed are distinct and specific to the given author, but there are two common characteristics in their feminist literary approaches to war. Each author protests war: war is destructive and perverse for Barnes, traumatic for H.D., and disruptive for Stein. Additionally, each author, to varying degrees, depicts female bodies as markers of presence in war narrative. The female body stands in as a textual marker or symbol of female identity. From my perspective any literary representation of the female body in a war narrative functions as an insistence on and indication of presence in both the text and in the world outside of the book. All of the authors in this study seek to write about war by creating space in narratives that accommodate female characters and female authors as well as by foregrounding female views and experiences that have traditionally been foreclosed. When these authors write about women in war, they write women into war narrative and thus claim authority for women to tell their stories. The female body becomes the primary vehicle for a textual insistence on women's place in war text.

In general the authors in this study are concerned with women's bodies and gender politics. These concerns manifest themselves in treatments of trauma (as it pertains to female bodies and bodies in general) and in a protest against war (usually in relation to gender politics). In order to protest war and draw attention to trauma suffered by female subjects, the authors evoke corporeal representations. These corporeal depictions are often grounded in the author's personal experience or connect in another way to the author's own body. The authors are able to insert female characters into war writing by etching a place for themselves within the text.

In *Nightwood* the characters are based upon actual people Barnes knew, but her own body is noticeably absent. Barnes is unable to represent human female bodies fully in connection to war in most instances. Instead, she relies on animals' bodies and inanimate objects to communicate female trauma and suffering. Barnes did not possess the firsthand knowledge of war that H.D. and Stein possessed by virtue of living in Europe during World War I and World War II; they could witness and write their own bodies and experiences into their literary works in ways that Barnes, who was distanced from World War I and left Europe before seeing much of World War II, could.

H.D. and Stein were able to insert and actualize female bodies into their war writing fully because they drew upon their own corporeal experiences as women who lived in Europe during both wars—and they had literary precedents upon whose work they could build and expand. H.D. refers to herself as a poet-prophet and references her survivor status throughout *Tril-*

ogy, and Stein's war writing is a testament to the realities she faced and the mind-set she assumed in wartime. The ways in which the selected authors depict female bodies vary according to personal experience of war and according to the author's artistic treatment in her approach to war.

The selected authors may possess different strategies in representing women and war, but the authors share in modernist stylistic innovation. Formal experimentation occupies a place within the project of rewriting war narrative. In more ways than one the modernist authors featured in this study were trying to make literature new. Perhaps the most obvious manner in which Barnes, H.D., and Stein experimented is in literary form. As avant-garde writers who desired to write technically challenging and artistically powerful works, each of the writers in this study contributed innovative literature to the modernist catalogue. Working within surrealism Barnes depicts nightmarish episodes in her dense prose to underscore the traumas suffered by her main characters in *Nightwood*. H.D. incorporates her early Imagist experiments in the epic *Trilogy*, and the result is a long, cryptic poem that relies on crystalline images and epic references to myths, history, biblical narratives, and autobiography. Stein is probably best known for her experiments with language. In her efforts to revitalize language and infuse words with new meanings, the syntax in the novel *Mrs. Reynolds* is unconventional, and meaning is often artfully obscured. There is something transgressive about experimentation; experimentation signals a break with tradition and convention. These women writers were transgressive in both what they chose to depict and how they chose to depict it. Making the personal political and insisting on female presence and sometimes female corporeal suffering during wartime are transgressive literary and sociohistorical acts.[1]

In writing about war and trauma, the authors were treating relatively new subjects for women writers, and their modernist stylistic preferences highlight their content choices. Experimentation might be a necessary element for circumventing the silence of foreclosure; it draws attention to forgotten or discarded subjects and ideas in a manner that is new and exciting (because unfamiliar). Approaching sensitive subjects in an artistically challenging fashion may also allow the writer distance and thus the ability to circumvent silence induced by trauma. It is important to note that the selected writers in this study experienced war-related fear and hardship to varying degrees. Both Barnes and H.D. suffered breakdowns attributed to war, and Stein admits to being fearful occasionally, though most of her energy is spent in maintaining a brave appearance. It is significant and noteworthy that Barnes, H.D., and Stein create characters and opportunities that allow them to speak trauma. In *Nightwood* Matthew O'Connor and Nora Flood model the practice of psychoanalysis, the "talking cure." H.D. returns to her World War I novel at Freud's behest and writes out her trauma in *Bid Me to Live*. And Stein suspects that her concentrated writing during World War II was an exercise to keep her mind occupied and diverted from the realities of occupation. She writes out her fears, masked in a playful tone, in her autobiographical works. Stein's fictional character Mrs. Reynolds talks out her fears about death and relocation to her husband in moments when the text shows Mrs. Reynolds unable to suppress her recurring and sometimes debilitating fear. These female authors capitalize on experimentation, such as modernist stylistic and generic innovations and the incorporation of psychoanalytic tendencies such as the talking cure, to make new the problems and situations pertaining to women and war and trauma, thereby drawing attention to important gender and identity issues.

In terms of experimentation there is a clear arc from Barnes to H.D. to Stein. Each author in this study is a product of her place in literary and social history, and I position each writer by what I see as her literary and historical agenda and by the relationship of her work to the visibility and status of women and the woman writer. The strategy each writer uses in representing war and trauma bespeaks her place in what I see as a genealogy of female American modernist women war writers. In short what these modernist female authors offer are multiple narratives that rewrite generic patriarchal war narratives in an experimental and feminist fashion.

Theoretical Framework

In this study I am engaged in investigating the representations of war and trauma in relation to American women's lives on the British and French home fronts during World War I and World War II. I found it helpful to take what I classify broadly as a feminist, poststructuralist approach because the war literature of Barnes, H.D., and Stein has been rejected by phallogocentrism, or male textual bias. Little critical attention has been paid to the way these writers represent women and war within the selected texts I will examine, and these authors and their war works have never been considered together in a single study.[2] The logocentric argument leveled at female civilian writers is that they could not have any realistic or significant experience of war; to find authentic accounts of trauma, one must turn to male combatants or men who had more knowledge of war and war-related trauma than women, simply because they are men. The trauma induced by war, not to mention war itself, has long been considered a male problem. I maintain instead that female authors have valuable contributions to make to war and trauma literature; oftentimes these authors expose false binary relationships while also illustrating the trauma and suffering experienced by women on the home front. In addition, I contend that female authors depict active female survivors of war to counter the phallogocentric bias in linguistic, narrative, and authorial notions of war as a man's experience or activity, thereby effectively positioning war within the sphere of the domestic to illustrate a differently gendered experience of war than what traditional binary constructions of war (e.g., war/peace, frontlines/home front, male/female, active/passive, or shell shock/hysteria) would have us believe. I wish to draw attention to women's representations of war and trauma not only to show that women did write about these subjects but also to illustrate how writers such as Barnes, H.D., and Stein dismantle binary oppositions that construct women as invisible or passive and untouched by war suffering or trauma when depicted in literary treatments of war. And, although I construct a genealogy to trace the development of women's war writing with my selected writers, the literary work produced by these writers is very different. There is not a single text or episode that can be reified as *the* female war experience; rather, I think of this literature as participating in a larger conversation of identity politics: how are war representations and experiences gendered, and who has the authority to write about them? I do, however, want to validate women's presence in war narrative, and, because poststructuralism does not privilege experience, I draw on embodiment theory in order to shape my discussion of women's experiences of war.

From here I will profile the theorists and significant concepts that have guided my thinking about this project and informed the theoretical framework that is sometimes explicit and sometimes implicit in the body of the study. I will define key terms and highlight the ideas that underpin the following chapters. In particular I draw from the following theorists: Dominick LaCapra (trauma studies), Judith Butler (poststructuralism), Elaine Scarry (war rhetoric and ideology), Elizabeth Grosz (embodiment theory), and Jacques Derrida (deconstruction).

I frame my theoretical understanding of the politics of trauma and identity primarily using LaCapra's *Writing History, Writing Trauma.* In particular I find his approaches to trauma innovative and applicable to an investigation of the intersection of trauma and subjectivity. I understand trauma through my reading of LaCapra's work to be an emotional and/or psychological wound with emotional and psychological effects that plague the survivor until they are worked through. I do not attempt, however, to ascertain to what extent characters have been traumatized in this study. Instead, I focus primarily on representations of trauma and the identity politics therein, and I find LaCapra's concept of "founding trauma" useful in examining the characters in the literary works of the selected authors.

LaCapra elucidates his notion of founding trauma as one that "becomes the basis of an identity" (161). The characters in Barnes's *Nightwood*, the persona of H.D.'s *Trilogy*, and the main character in Stein's *Mrs. Reynolds* struggle with founding traumas to varying degrees. In these works the characters attempt to work through and make sense of trauma or traumatic episodes and their own place within an exclusionary and gendered society. Barnes concentrates on exploring the practices and structures of difference and exclusion, and she ultimately links alterity with traumatic responses to war and difference in the years between the two world wars. H.D.'s work assumes the notion of founding trauma as the impetus for further and nuanced explorations into female suffering and recovery. Stein reaffirms her own and her characters' responses to traumatic war situations in several texts, although her tone often obscures an emotional involvement. But there are places in Stein's works in which readers are offered a glimpse into the latent fear and suffering that impact responses to war activity on the home front. While I read trauma as shaping the identity of the characters in the various works I discuss, I also recognize that depictions of traumatized female bodies are fraught with political implications related to gendered identity. Gender matters in representations of trauma. The selected authors address identity politics in their representations of war and trauma, culminating in depictions of traumatized female bodies.

LaCapra defines "identity politics" inductively when he examines the challenges of studying political attitudes and positions that exhibit the concerns of different social groups. He understands identity politics as involving "a grid of subject positions," and the problem is that one "remains within that grid" through "processes of identification or excessive objectification." He laments that one's subject position often remains unchallenged and unchanged as a result of the rigidity of defined subject positions. As I see it, the aim of studying identity politics is to identify the markers, structures, or behaviors (brought about by discursive formations) that construct and perhaps limit one's agency or perspective in order to better understand a subject and the subject's (or one's own) place in the world in relation to others. According to LaCapra, the challenge of such study "is somehow to try to test critically, perhaps in certain ways validate, or perhaps transform one's subject position, so that one doesn't end up where one began" (175). Ideally, scholarship on identity construction and identity politics should open up avenues to understanding and transformation (or acceptance) of other subject positions. One approach to the study of identity politics is poststructural analysis.

My approach to writing about and thinking about identity construction involves an acknowledgment of identity as discursively formed, meaning that identity is informed by and construed in language. In *Bodies That Matter* Butler contends that "the occupation of the name is that by which one is, quite without choice, situated within discourse" (122). For Butler one's identity is somewhat constrained and certainly positioned within discourse ("interpellated"), but there remains some space to manipulate identity by engaging with the binary oppositions that construct "I." According to Butler, "The 'I' who would oppose its constructions is always in some sense drawing from that construction to articulate its oppositions; further, the 'I' draws what is called its 'agency' in part through being implicated in the very relations of power that it seeks to oppose" (122–23). In other words, Butler sees the "I" as able to engage in playing with and articulating binary structures but already and always grounded in the very power play and terms one wants to oppose. But the ability to articulate and manipulate and thus disrupt binary constructions in order to display power relations, even while implicated, is an enlightening and exciting project—one in which my study shows Barnes, H.D., and Stein participating.

Identity politics for Butler relies on "identity-claims as rallying points for political mobilization." She explains that these claims "appear to hold the promise of unity, solidarity, universality" (*Bodies* 188). While "identity-claims" may differ within a given group associated under a single term, the appearance of a community strengthens the group's ability to raise awareness of certain problems affecting the community and, on a very basic level, to build and enlarge upon the profile of the group in order to insist upon presence and acknowledgment. Thus, as I see it, identity politics is an important topic for academic research because the discussions and examinations of identities in relation to power can have real-world ramifications. With increased focus and discussion the possibilities for the cultural intelligibility of marginalized groups (the sometimes culturally unintelligible) are opened up, especially because Butler observes that signifiers that designate subject positions "are empty signs which come to bear phantasmatic investments of various kinds." There is room to rewrite terms because there cannot be a universal origin, or Truth, and the signifier is "open-ended and performative" (191).

Studying the ways in which binary oppositions structure identity enables one to articulate and address issues pertaining to visibility and agency. Consigning ideological formations to a "*re*articulation" leaves "open the production of new subject-positions, new political signifiers, and new linkages to become the rallying points for politicization" (Butler, *Bodies* 193). The "subject-position" of women, for instance, "is never fixed by the signifier 'women'"; rather, it "is perpetually renegotiated and rearticulated in relation to other signifiers within the political field" (195), and we can see this renegotiation and rearticulation play out in the selected works by Barnes, H.D., and Stein in regard to what it means to be a woman during wartime (or in the years between war) and how, in fact, women and female bodies can suffer and cope. Butler remarks, "To ameliorate and rework this violence [wrought by a concept or description that forecloses further discussion or investigation but that aspires to be impartial and comprehensive], it is necessary to learn a double movement: to invoke the category and, hence, provisionally to institute an identity and at the same time to open the category as a site of permanent political contest" (222). This double movement is precisely the performance Barnes, H.D., and Stein enact. They gesture to categorical feminine identity and redefine it by ascribing new performances and components. In H.D.'s work, for example, this poststructuralist erasure of binary categories is crucial to the reclamation of a liberatory position. It is through refusing the virgin/harlot distinction upheld by the binary opposition of the Virgin Mary and Mary Magdalene that H.D. constructs and privileges a female figure who is both physical and spiritual, sinner and saint, and who, therefore, can enact the kind of earthly and spiritual healing she views as necessary.

Different kinds of behavior are possible for women or men, but "gender transformation" requires "a different sort of repeating," a "breaking or subversive repetition" (Butler, "Performative Acts" 402). In other words, gender identity correlates with sanctioned (repeated without the threat of punishment) performances or behavior, but there are opportunities and potential for subversion "through a series of acts which are renewed, revised, and consolidated through time" (406). Butler cautions that gender and cultural codes are "not passively scripted" on the body (410); instead, they are assumed. The acting out of a set of "stylized repetition of acts" forms and assigns gender identity. The authors I discuss in the following chapters challenge notions of gender and gendered behavior in connection with war by enacting what Butler calls "gender transformation": while alluding to stylized repetitions of acts, they enact subversive repetitions that allow the feminized body to speak out trauma to varying degrees. The authors approach the gendered body from what Butler describes as a "feminist point of view": feminists "reconceive the gendered body as the legacy of sedimented acts rather than a predetermined or foreclosed structure, essence, or fact, whether natural, cultural, or linguistic" (406). As such, the selected authors mark the characters in feminized ways and typically locate their actions in domestic scenes so that we know they are female, but the authors also deconstruct the binary constructions that prevent women from acknowledging war trauma or responding to war.

In *The Body in Pain: The Making and Unmaking of the World* Elaine Scarry foregrounds the perverse purpose of war: injuring. The women writers in this study protest war, and they protest, among other things, the business of injury that Scarry highlights as the main objective of war, even though war rhetoric attempts to obfuscate it. Citizens and bodies, both soldier and civilian, are unmade through war activity. The soldier is unmade as a good citizen because he is sanctioned to kill, a criminal act in peacetime. As Scarry explains, "The act of killing, motivated by care 'for the nation,' is a deconstruction of the state as it ordinarily manifests itself in the body." The soldier "consents to 'unmake' himself, deconstruct himself, empty himself of civil content" (121–22).

The male pronoun is used throughout by Scarry to refer to soldiers, thus positioning warfare within the province of male activity. She reads the unmaking of bodies as an act of deconstruction; bodies are emptied of meaning, and meaning is consequently destabilized. Civilian bodies are also unmade and deconstructed through injury and death. Scarry offers commonplace examples of the unmaking of civilian bodies through injury and death: arms no longer gesture; hands no longer play piano; fingers and palms no longer know the weight of tools or how to use them; feet can no longer pedal a bicycle; and bodies no longer dance. As bodies are deconstructed physically through injury, what Scarry terms as "civilization" is unmade (122–23). As simple as these observations (e.g., war is a perverse endeavor that aims to injure, kill, and unmake bodies) appear, they are displaced by war rhetoric, omissions, and faulty perceptions (64). Consequently, the selected works of Barnes, H.D., and Stein are noteworthy in their discerning and perceptive perspectives; they protest war because they understand that "the main purpose and outcome of war is injuring" (63). These women writers also view and protest war as a patriarchal enterprise that acknowledges and validates only the pain and suffering of men.

Barnes situates war almost squarely within male experience, writing women into the periphery of war narrative. For the most part Barnes's *Nightwood* cannot assign women the agency to speak about war. And yet she attempts to bring women and feminized bodies into her portrayals of war's effects on the domestic economy. She protests the violence wrought by men in battle, and she depicts war as an injury-producing enterprise. In *Nightwood* Barnes offers Matthew O'Connor and Robin Vote as her victims of a patriarchal enterprise that enlists men like O'Connor to make them "men" and denies women like Robin any claim to war-related suffering. H.D. and Stein also contest war as the province of male experience, but both writers insert female characters as the principal players in their epic and novel treatments of war. They turn their attentions to writing new versions of war narratives that pivot on female perspectives. The poet-prophet in *Trilogy* can descry and decry the politics of injury in relation to women; the poet-prophet/H.D. enacts a healing process that encompasses multiple women and their stories and ultimately sanctions acknowledgment of war-related suffering and validation of female presence in wartime and in various narratives. Stein's *Mrs. Reynolds* privileges the voice and reflections of a female civilian during World War II. Mrs. Reynolds occasionally alludes to her fear of injury and to deportation, but she is mostly concerned with managing her home and the work that entails. As such, Stein creates a novel that focuses on an aspect of war, the home front economy, and a perspective of war, that of the female civilian, that protests and contests female absence in generic patriarchal war narratives.

Elizabeth Grosz's *Volatile Bodies: Toward a Corporeal Feminism* explores "embodiment" and the implications for feminist study of embodiment theory. I use Grosz's discussions to orient and ground my thinking and use of *embodiment* throughout this project. In turn the theoretical work of Maurice Merleau-Ponty influences Grosz's understanding of the concept. Grosz spends a significant amount of time clarifying Merleau-Ponty's position on embodiment, and this exercise allows her to clarify her own position as well. For Merleau-Ponty, as for Grosz, *embodiment* refers to the interconnected relationship between corporeality and consciousness. Grosz explains: "Insofar as I live the body, it is a phenomenon experienced by me and thus provides the very horizon and perspectival point which places me in the world and makes relations between me, other objects, and other subjects possible. It is the body as I live it, as I experience it, and as it shapes my experience that Merleau-Ponty wishes to elucidate" (86). Information is perceived and received from and about the world through bodies, and, because she subscribes to Merleau-Ponty's version of phenomenology, Grosz refuses to divorce the female body from embodied experience.

In this conception lived experience resonates in meaningful ways because experience is processed through corporeality and the mind. Corporeality, consciousness, and lived experience are the three components that make up embodiment for Grosz, and the manner in which I refer to embodiment points to and derives from this conception of it. Neither Merleau-

Ponty nor Grosz is interested in reductionism or the bifurcation associated with binary oppositions, and both attempt to destabilize such constructions.

Incorporating Grosz, and by extension Merleau-Ponty, I synthesize embodiment theory with poststructuralist theory; as such, I incorporate discussions of the selected authors' experiences of war when appropriate in the following chapters to refine and enlarge upon my feminist, poststructuralist readings of their representations of war and trauma. The selected authors' experience and observations of war permeate their literary output; perhaps they focus on bodies in their texts to underscore and draw a correlation to actual lived experience (even if not their own). Experience for Merleau-Ponty and Grosz "is always necessarily embodied, corporeally constituted" (95). Barnes based her characters in *Nightwood* on actual people, and there are direct correlations between the lived experiences of H.D. and Stein in their respective war texts.

Jacques Derrida's *Of Grammatology*—namely its relation to logocentrism and its concepts have influenced my understanding of deconstruction and, more broadly, feminist, poststructuralist theory in relation to this project. Grosz notes that many feminists "regard logocentrism as inherently complicit with phallocentrism" (94). Similarly, I prefer the term *phallogocentrism* because it emphasizes sexual difference in the role of language and usage more than the term *phallocentrism*, which suggests male bias without recourse to language conventions. Phallogocentrism speaks to the patriarchal structures in language, in generic conventions, and in the social world that the selected authors come up against. What Barnes, H.D., and Stein engage and take issue with in language and narrative is a logocentric system that is dominated by male bodies, male concepts, and male presence. In other words, we have been so constructed by the language and logic of a system that we often take for granted what seems to us to be commonsense or true, but this situation is what prompts or prepares Barnes, H.D., and Stein to stage literary and social interventions.

Literary and Social Interventions in Women's War Writing

While modernist scholars have assumed the task of recovering female authors, there is much work still to do, especially in light of how female modernist writers experienced and treated through experimental forms and embodied language the violence they confronted in the modern world. Regardless of combatant status, men and women were subjected to the trauma of a changing world that threatened lives through the duration of two world wars. As such, the personal and the political spheres became entangled, and several important female poets and novelists conflated issues assigned to femininity with the most masculine and most political enterprise of all: war. Barnes, H.D., and Stein embrace aspects of traditional feminine identities that had become denigrated or marginalized (i.e., emotional responses, domestic affiliation, female embodiment, and women's identity issues), but at the same time they challenge and reinvent representations of women and war for modernist literature by imagining new identities for women that were shaped by the conditions of living in a female body in the first half of the twentieth century. A new body of war literature emerged, one in which a feminist investigation of war, trauma, and identity politics countered the paradigmatic war experience narrated by men. This study is the first to consider representations of war, trauma, and gender within the collective work of Barnes, H.D., and Stein.

This project does not focus on these women writers' social and literary interventions in matters of sexuality. All three writers were bisexual or homosexual, and this difference matters in terms of their identity politics, broadly speaking. I provide discussions of sexuality when it is especially pertinent to the scope of this study (e.g., Barnes's *Nightwood* and Stein's *Lifting Belly*), but, outside of these two works, I do not find that sexuality impinges on the writers' strategies for writing about war in a striking or significant manner. Yet, just as these women writers' whiteness surely factors into their worldviews, their sexual preferences are inextricably linked to their ideological positions. I suspect that these writers were acutely conscious of their doubly disenfranchised status, as we see in Barnes's protestation late in her life that she was not a lesbian. Barnes, H.D., and Stein occupied marginal positions in mainstream society because of their sex and sexual orientation, and so they really are, in that sense, the perfect writers to tackle representations of war, trauma, female identity, and embodiment, all of which are marginalized and dismissed in canonical literature. By virtue of their subject positions they might be more aware of the ethical necessity for female civilians and female writers to enter into the conversation(s) about war and trauma, a subject that had been appropriated by heterosexual narratives and policed by men. Because war is the great modernist subject, the poverty of canonical war literature by women distances them from greatness in political ways, namely in the form of canonization and validation (i.e., who is allowed to write about war and trauma and thus who can legitimately suffer).

As Rita Felski observes, male experience and male writing have long been the paradigmatic modernist text. The feminist project of recovering important female writers and writing must include work that engages with women's experiences and perspectives, thereby presenting a bigger and more accurate panorama of responses to modernity. Felski asks: "How would our understanding of modernity change if instead of taking male experience as paradigmatic, we were to look instead at texts written primarily by or about women? And what if feminine phenomena, often seen as having a secondary or marginal status, were given a central importance in the analysis of the culture of modernity? What *difference* would such a procedure make?" (10). The difference would be revolutionary: women's experience would be valued and included as important, artistic, and critical: new viewpoints and recovered texts would necessarily emerge. The identity of modern women writers is so violently circumscribed that, in order to produce war literature, women have had to circumvent both stultifying literary and social conventions and bias, all the while carving out a place for themselves on the battlefield of identity politics. Indeed, the exclusion of women from the status of canonical war writing is still rampant: canonical collections of war poetry and war writing have historically elided women.[3]

Perhaps a reason for the marginalization of the selected authors is due to their engagement with sentimentalism. The feminine body in the domestic economy is closely associated with the sentimental, and Barnes, H.D., and Stein made use of feminine-coded issues and concerns but did so in experimental ways that circumvented the twentieth-century detractions of sentimental or woman-identified nineteenth-century literature. Suzanne Clark's *Sentimental Modernism: Women Writers and the Revolution of the Word* clarifies the problem encountered by avant-garde modernist women writers when she declares that "the modernist revolution turned away from ordinary language and everyday life. This disconnection from social consequence, from history, has everything to do with the gendering of intellectuality. . . . A crisis emerges from the rejection of narratives that have explained and legitimated feeling" (3). In fact, Barnes, H.D., and Stein did turn away from conventional forms and language, but their responses to war and trauma are gendered because they treat social consequence and history within a framework of sentimental concerns and issues with feeling. In particular, they focus on the appearance or threat of tragedy in the domestic sphere, with a focus on women's identity issues.

With the emergence of modernism, Clark notes, the influence of women's writing was discredited (1). The female body was eradicated from the text in order to shift the focus to the body of the text itself, becoming more and more an impersonal, impervious, and masculine construct. Formalism or new criticism reigned, rather than a subjective or embodied theoretical school. Clark argues that "the developing new criticism [of formalism] did not promote female reputations" because "the sentimental acts as a pivotal ground in a battle over literary and moral value, over the fundamental social warrants constructing discursive agreements." The formalist approach, as Clark maintains, has historically distanced and alienated women writers and the sentimental from the modernist canon. Conversely, a critical approach that takes into account language construction, the female body, and trauma would better serve the female modernist texts in which an understanding of the role of language, marked bodies, and war has been eradicated. Attention to embodiment issues in modernist texts enables the female body to be written back into critical discussions. Clark further argues that the repressed sentimental sensibility "also calls up the repressed involvement of literature with power—literature as a rhetorical instrument, literature used in the interests of economy and politics, literature as locus of pleasure and transgression" (2). The works selected for this study precisely illustrate the feminist interests of the authors in rhetoric, economies, and politics as well as serving as sites of transgressions.

In the chapter on Barnes and *Nightwood* I discuss the author's sensitivity to war trauma in connection with feminized bodies during the years between the two world wars. War is the subtext in *Nightwood* that cryptically suggests why the characters behave the way they do and serves as a rationale for a strange, animalistic, and depraved world. The war has left its stamp on two major characters, Robin Vote (a bisexual woman) and Matthew O'Connor (a male homosexual transvestite).

And yet Barnes cannot quite figure out how to represent women and war in her work. The representations of female trauma and suffering female bodies are couched in proxies in *Nightwood.* Female bodies are substituted with animal bodies and an inanimate object. Barnes exposes the circumscription of suffering female bodies; in *Nightwood* she successfully illustrates Robin's inability (or the text's inability) to discuss pain or articulate the nature of her trauma, which is presumably related to World War I. Other characters can talk about suffering, namely O'Connor and Nora Flood. O'Connor, in fact, is the character who tells all of the stories about war. O'Connor consoles Nora about being miserable with an allusion to his participation in World War I and to his personal struggle as a societal outsider: "My war brought me many things; let yours bring you as much" (109). War is O'Connor's topic as a biological man, even though he enlists in the army as a remedy or punishment for his homosexual identity and purported feminized body. While O'Connor counsels Nora about her non-war-related trauma in war terms, the shell-shocked body of Robin is unable to speak about its wounds until the very end of the novel. In fact, Robin says very little in the text at all until she suffers a breakdown, and, even then, her vocalization is extralinguistic. Her barking is noted in the text, but her meaning does not register. Her animal vocalization, however, speaks volumes; Robin's trauma is left unacknowledged and untreated, and she consequently devolves into an animalistic state. Her voice has been rendered mute, and psychologically she is damaged, but O'Connor is the only one who can reference war and articulate stories about it. As a (fraudulent) doctor and veteran, O'Connor possesses the only authorized voice in the text that can discuss trauma. Robin, on the other hand, is excluded from acknowledgment, and her voice is marginalized as a result.

Part of the lesson O'Connor imparts to Nora is the recognition of war experience as something relevant and meaningful to her experience as a woman; he offers his war stories and observations to Nora as a means for her to better understand and contextualize her relationship with Robin. *Nightwood* supplies a surrealistic account of the exclusion of women from war narrative. The novel protests war as perverse, contrary to what is morally right or good. War, as the injury-producing business of extermination, emerges as one of two perverted practices that are protested by O'Connor. The other perverted practice he rails against is the extermination of difference by society.

The next chapter provides an examination of a more pronounced artistic rendition of women within war narrative. H.D.'s work witnesses female war trauma through allusions to the author's own experiences. Witnessing provides a personal statement about lived experience and, as such, witnessing is a very powerful and political act because it validates and legitimizes a perspective on reality. H.D., unlike Barnes, could speak to the civilian conditions in Europe during World War I and II. Being in London provided her with a firsthand account of war. In fact, she endured the greatest personal suffering during the world wars of the selected authors. Freud encouraged her to write out her trauma and record it in a narrative, and *Bid Me to Live* (1960), a roman à clef, served this purpose. It is in *Trilogy*, however, that H.D. presents her epic vision of trauma and healing; *Bid Me to Live* cannot get past its insular perspective on trauma.

In the very beginning of *Trilogy* the violence and trauma of war are vividly, if cryptically, depicted. "The Walls Do Not Fall" is primarily concerned with offering pictures of violence and delving into the trauma inflicted by war:

> the bone-frame was made for
> no such shock knit within terror,
> yet the skeleton stood up to it: the flesh? it was melted away,
> the heart burnt out, dead ember,
> tendons, muscles shattered, outer husk dismembered,
> yet the frame held: we passed the flame: we wonder
> what saved us? what for?
> (4)

The tone of a shell-shocked female civilian emerges clearly: the human body is subjected to bombardments, or "shock knit within terror," and, consequently, the body is metaphorically dismembered and the heart, a metaphor for emotional feeling, is incapacitated. But the civilian talks herself into strength and survival as she searches for a purpose to her life amid destruction ("yet the frame held: we passed the flame: we wonder / what saved us? what for?"). Unlike *Bid Me to Live, Trilogy* considers avenues toward healing. H.D. positions and celebrates sundry women (and their bodies) in *Trilogy* as salvation figures as part of its panoramic and mythological response to trauma and exclusion. If Barnes offers a dystopian view of the world between the two wars, then H.D. offers a utopian vision as a promise of salvation. Indeed, *Trilogy* upholds the poet-prophet, a female visionary poet, as the ultimate salvation figure in the second section of *Trilogy*, "Tribute to the Angels." The poet-prophet advocates wholeness and peace, and she sanctions multiple female identities and performances as praiseworthy. H.D. assumes the role of the poet-prophet to reclaim and venerate marginalized mythological and biblical women and their stories.

In "The Flowering of the Rod," the third section of *Trilogy*, H.D. presents an alternative to male, linear, and traditional narratives that leave women out and prevent them access to their own stories, whether through reception or authorship. H.D. writes women into a palimpsestic design (she conflates the mother figure, the holy lady and the unwritten book, the poet, goddesses, Mary of Bethlehem, and Mary Magdalene in order to redeem and venerate one and all) to foster the wholeness espoused by the poet-prophet. H.D. offers Mary Magdalene as a gift (in the form of myrrh in the poem) who will enable healing and inclusion from trauma and exclusion. "I am Mary, a great tower; / through my will and my power, / Mary shall be myrrh" (135). H.D.'s work constitutes a feminist critique of war and circumscription as well as a critique of male dominance in literature and narrative. The palimpsestic design of *Trilogy* fosters wholeness and creates a space for healing narratives that include and foreground women and their contributions. Rather than serving as a marginal or denigrated figure, as she does in biblical narrative, Mary Magdalene becomes a principal character, and her story is imaginatively "recovered" by H.D. In short H.D. privileges female characters and their stories in *Trilogy* in ways that the earlier modernist writing on war could not. Unlike works by Barnes, H.D. focuses exclusively on women in war (instead of placing them in the periphery or in the company of men) and models the actual rewriting of generic war narrative she agitates for in *Trilogy*. Additionally, H.D. depicts trauma and suffering in a much more personal fashion than Barnes, often referencing her own experience of war within such works as *Bid Me to Live* and *Trilogy*.

The third chapter is dedicated to Stein and her war texts, specifically the novel *Mrs. Reynolds*. Like H.D., Stein chronicles her impressions of World War I and World War II in her literary output, and she also insists on a personal, female perspective on war and domestic matters. Unlike H.D. or Barnes, Stein details the embodied state of the title character in *Mrs. Reynolds* in her recording of Mrs. Reynolds's daily experiences and her reactions to them. Stein also painstakingly documents her own conditions and mind-set in the autobiographical *Wars I Have Seen* (1945). This embrace of mundane details in reference to corporeality and consciousness carries through Stein's writings on war. We see Stein concerned with replicating a "historical . . . state of mind" in *Mrs. Reynolds* (331), but this concern permeates other works, including the long poem *Lifting Belly* (1953) and the dialogue *Brewsie and Willie* (1946). The pragmatic view that emerges from Stein's war writing is in stark contrast to H.D.'s horrified response, followed by her epic, utopian vision. But Stein's political situation was very different from H.D.'s. Although Stein lived in occupied France as a lesbian American Jew, she was strangely removed from war, due to the protection of Vichy friends, as she and her partner Alice B. Toklas lived a quiet existence in the French countryside. At issue for Stein during wartime were the daily concerns of securing food and news, which she catalogued in *Wars I Have Seen*. As a result, the women in Stein's war writing are construed as figures of endurance: they wait, endure minor hardships, and survive.

The epitome of a heroine for Stein (other than herself in *Wars I Have Seen*) is the titled heroine of *Mrs. Reynolds*. The novel lacks a traditional plot because of Stein's overpowering quotidian vision in the novel. All Mrs. Reynolds seems to do is track the passing of time when she is not otherwise occupied in conversing with passersby, relating a passing observation, or scouting for food—but she survives and becomes the heroine of her own war story. The focus of the novel is solely on Mrs. Reynolds's outlook, her physical welfare, and her daily routine. Stein transfers her own mind-set and experiences to Mrs. Reynolds and to the persona in *Lifting Belly*, but she diffuses her war knowledge to American soldiers in *Brewsie and Willie* as well. She capitalizes on opportunities to insert her personal knowledge and sometimes even herself into her war writing, thereby writing and constructing her own war narrative with allusions to her own embodiment.

Among Stein's fictional literary characters Mrs. Reynolds emerges as the most embodied female civilian because she possesses a conscious mind and active body that experience the world while she reflectively comments upon it all. The novel *Mrs. Reynolds* makes the personal political by highlighting and foregrounding the experience and person of its main character. The distinction between the outside world of war and the inside world of the home is cleverly obliterated by Stein in one of her most experimental novels. She avoids reductive binary relationships (i.e., men/women, active/passive, and war/peace) throughout the novel. Instead, Stein rends asunder the marked body (e.g., female, passive, and domestic) of Mrs. Reynolds and renders her above all capable and brave during wartime. She writes a woman into war narrative, creating a political space for a personal, domestic, and female response to war and trauma. For Mrs. Reynolds is afraid of all that war brings, and yet she perseveres and remains a "soldier" of the home front economy. The notion of women as active contributors values the work of women in the domestic sphere during wartime. Stein highlights this point: "Civilians said Mrs. Reynolds, I met a girl today her name was Ruth and I asked her just what you asked me and she said, one woman makes four soldiers, so what is a civilian and I said what is a civilian and now you ask me what is a civilian"(280). In case her privileging of women's courage, survival tactics, and wartime contributions went unheeded, Stein spells out for the reader one of the messages of *Mrs. Reynolds:* the semantics and values of war and wartime need to be revised to include the female civilian as a valued participant and contributor on the home front. In *Mrs. Reynolds* Stein counters the limited visibility and agency male narratives have offered women in the past.

Multiple narratives touching on representations of women and traumatic experiences need to exist and receive acknowledgment because they may validate and sanction real-world responses and experiences. In short, as Scarry also argues, the (literary) representations of trauma are imbued with power and political ramifications: "But the relative ease or difficulty with which that phenomenon can be *verbally represented* also influences the ease or difficulty with which that phenomenon comes to be *politically represented*" (12). Without cultural acknowledgment, sanction, or models with which they might identify, women writers can easily be disenfranchised from verbal representation and, by extension, political representation. The marginality of women's war writing correlates to how the signs of war writing and experience have been defined: as male experience and the subject of men's writing. As a result, the sign of war literature defined by and for men implies that only men can legitimately write about war or suffer from the trauma of war effects. Women are denied the opportunity either to respond to trauma during wartime or to find responses with which to identify afterward. They are also denied avenues toward healing because the work of healing can only take place when trauma is recognized and (re)actively approached.

In this study I analyze representations of war and trauma in embodied responses by Barnes, H.D., and Stein. I offer alternative discussions of female identities and bodies that have been traditionally circumscribed in scholarship on American modernist women's literature. The aim of this project is to present a more rounded picture of who was participating and what was being contested, reaffirmed, and synthesized in the realm of identity politics and women's modernist literature in the early twentieth century.

CHAPTER 1

Circumventing the Circumscription of Marginalization

Implicit Critiques of War and Trauma in Djuna Barnes's *Nightwood*

Djuna Barnes is unable to position war directly within the experience of female characters in her literary output because she did not experience World War I or World War II in the ways that H.D. or Gertrude Stein did and thus could not bear witness like they could in their work. Barnes spent World War I and the majority of World War II in the United States. She left Paris on October 24, 1939 (Barnes, "War in Paris" 269). And yet she captures her horror of the world in the aftermath of World War I in *Nightwood* (published in 1936 in England and 1937 in the United States) by rendering war, with its aims of injuring and destroying, as a perversion of civilization. When Barnes represents women in connection with war or war-related trauma, she does so by proxies, by analogies, and through allusions. Although she is unable to insert women fully into war episodes or give them agency to talk about war or trauma, Barnes is able to ascribe war knowledge and experience to feminized bodies, mainly in the forms of a homosexual man and various animals.

Nightwood communicates the political problems facing characters who harbor marginal (e.g., homosexual) identities during the years between World War I and World War II. The novel foregrounds the rhetoric of the extermination of difference that would ultimately shape the rhetoric of World War II in regard to homosexual and Jewish identity. These characters suffer from disenfranchisement and trauma, and this interconnected affliction is often couched in war-related terms, metaphors, or stories. In *Nightwood* Barnes casts war rhetoric and ideology as perverse in their insistence on forming marginal subjects, making them into scapegoats, and rendering them silent. I posit that *Nightwood* investigates identity politics within the framework of war and war tropes in order to politicize the traumas encountered in the modern world by embodied feminized subjects. The novel positions traumatic episodes within the experience of various subjects that stand in for women. In other words, trauma is experienced by feminized subjects; those subjects are effeminate men, female animals, and an artifact that is inscribed by or points to performances of femininity (i.e., the doll baby). *Nightwood* offers an embodied response to trauma that can profitably be read through a feminist, poststructuralist lens because Barnes critiques the perverse phallogocentric world that breeds world wars and persecutes and erases difference. A poststructuralist analysis brings this critical subtext of war and trauma to the surface by examining the language constituting textual representations and performances of identity.

The novel follows in surrealistic fashion the lives of several characters and the interactions among them in Paris: Felix Volkbein, Matthew O'Connor, Nora Flood, Robin Vote, and Jenny Petherbridge. Instead of a linear plot progression, *Nightwood* is mainly made up of stories, confidences, and observations that the characters relate to each other. The first main character introduced is the Jewish Felix, who is an outsider because of his ethnic heritage and his deceitful claim to aristocracy. He is neither a Christian nor a baron, although he purports to be both. The novel opens with Felix spending time in the company of other marginalized people, namely circus performers, O'Connor, and Nora.

O'Connor is a fraudulent gynecologist who assumes the position of confidant for Felix and Nora. He is a World War I veteran, and he is representative of both the subtext and main focus of the novel: war and homosexuality. Nora catches O'Connor dressed in drag in bed, clothed in a nightgown with his face made up and wearing a wig, presumably waiting for sexual services. From that point on there are no barriers between

O'Connor and Nora, and they establish a solid friendship, allowing Nora to confide in O'Connor on several occasions. Nora's confessions to O'Connor constitute therapy: "I'm so miserable, Matthew, I don't know how to talk, and I've got to. I've got to talk to somebody. I can't live this way" (109). To be sure, O'Connor breaks down under the burden of serving as confidant to Felix and Nora: he may not be personally experiencing their trauma, but he empathizes with their pain. Nora's suffering is a result of her romantic involvement with Robin; she becomes unwittingly and unhappily involved in a love triangle concerning herself, Robin, and Jenny, the details of which become an obsession for Nora and thus the primary subject matter of her conversations and thoughts.

As for Robin, she is a sleepwalker; her trauma is tied to the nightmarish qualities in the chapter titled after her, "La Somnambule," but the source of her trauma is not stated explicitly, as is the practice of the narrative technique of *Nightwood* as a whole. Inferences can be made, and critiques are always implicit rather than explicit in the novel. Robin refrains from confiding in anyone, and she is depicted as traumatized (Nora claims that "in her [Robin's] death . . . she [Robin] has forgotten me" [109]) and metaphorically lost (O'Connor rhetorically asks, "Isn't it bitter enough for Robin that she is lost somewhere . . . ?" [105]). She wanders the streets at night, self-medicating through sex and alcohol, while Nora waits at their shared home for her to return. Robin seems incapable of healing; she appears damned to wander aimlessly, needlessly hurting her lovers and herself. The novel closes with Robin suffering a breakdown and devolving into an animalistic state, with Nora watching helplessly. Before her breakdown, Robin is briefly married to Felix; she gives birth to their son, Guido, and abandons them both for a relationship with Nora. Robin also has an affair with Jenny, who is referred to as a squatter; Jenny wrongfully moves in on Nora's girlfriend because she wants what other people have, but she is also obsessed with Robin although hurt by her.

Everyone suffers in *Nightwood*, and the suffering is invoked by war references and metaphors. World War I is the subtext and context by which the trauma of marginal characters is expressed; war is construed as perverse through the descriptions of battle, casualties, and the subsequent effects on effeminate soldiers (O'Connor and MacClusky) and a female civilian

(Robin). Additionally, although Barnes could not have realized the degree to which marginalized people would be persecuted and excised from society during World War II, each character in *Nightwood* possesses an identity that is already a liability due to racist and homophobic notions that circumscribe the identities of people such as Felix, O'Connor, Robin, Nora, and Jenny. Due to their outsider status, these characters, especially O'Connor and Nora, band together and attempt to work through war and non-war-related trauma in the aftermath of World War I, while Robin, as the shell-shocked civilian, inhabits a world that does not acknowledge her pain and renders her trauma inarticulate for the most part. As such, war is the subtext that frames and informs the representations of trauma in *Nightwood*.

The characters Barnes presents in *Nightwood* are all subjects outside of dominant discourses, subjects who befriend each other because of their outsider status. The identities associated with alterity—lesbian, Jewish, transvestite—are perverse (deviant) only in their relation to a truly perverse (corrupt) society that is preoccupied with war and the extermination of difference.[1]

A Study in Perversion: War, Trauma, and Exclusionary Politics in *Nightwood*

Writing to Barnes about *Nightwood*, T. R. Smith, Barnes's editor at Boni and Liveright, comments, "It is obvious to me that you tried to do an honest study of perversion but I am afraid you got lost in your studies" (qtd. in Herring 222–23). *Nightwood*'s "abnormal" style correlates to the grotesque realities encountered by deviant characters in the aftermath of a world war (Carlston 50). The abnormal treatment mimics the subtexts embedded in the novel: the perversity of war and the perversion of exclusionary politics and practices that aim to marginalize, erase, and exterminate difference and feminized responses to trauma.

War constitutes a perverted act in that its aim is to remake a socialized and law-abiding male citizen into a killing machine, as discussed in Elaine Scarry's criticism. The point that I want to make here, however, is my understanding of war rhetoric and activity as perverse in the insistence on gendered behavior in *Nightwood*: women are the outsiders, the subjects of alterity who are not allowed to speak about war or articulate war trauma because they are not fully interpellated into texts or discourse communities. They are not acknowledged as subjects who experienced war. Women could not participate in World War I in the way men could because of the gender binaries that divided men from women and prevented the blurring of boundaries pertaining to sexual identity. The realities of war were frightening enough without having sexual identities come completely unhinged: military service "was a male preserve. Women in military uniform were described as 'aping' men, which was not encouraged" (Goldman, Gledhill, and Hattaway 16). As a result, women were denied space in war narratives, and their suffering cannot be represented or legitimized in traditional patriarchal war narrative because, while women lived through a war, they did not go to war. Broadly, *Nightwood* exposes binary oppositions as based in exclusionary politics that are grounded in assumptions about gender and performances of it. Rather than reverse the binary relationships at play in discourses on war and identity, Barnes creates scenes that subtly erode the legitimacy of a simple binary construction to explain or enforce gendered behavior and speech in relation to war.

War informs *Nightwood,* a novel written between two world wars, to such an extent that I classify it as a war novel. It is very much a novel about trauma, trauma informed by and set against the backdrop of war. When a character asks O'Connor what will happen in the next few years, he replies: "Nothing . . . as always. We all go down in battle and we all come home" (274).[2] O'Connor may reference soldiers in his use of *we,* but he also alludes to others like himself: outsiders, people who are made to feel that they do not belong. Among those who are outsiders in *Nightwood* are O'Connor, a combat veteran who is a transvestite and fraudulent gynecologist (and only went to war to prove his suspect manhood); a shell-shocked lesbian civilian; and displaced Jewish characters. War and alterity are inextricably linked.

Barnes considers war in relation to women in her notes toward her memoir, which was never completed. She ponders the trauma of war on the home front in much the same elliptical fashion that she figures it in *Nightwood* in relation to Robin and O'Connor's animal stories. She begins, "It started with a high fever, and it ended with a war" (263). I read the subject as sickness, both personal sickness and a global sickness that manifested war and its perversities. Barnes equates her World War II experience in retrospect with terror, sickness, and entrapment. She contributes an observation concerning women on the home front: "Shaking silently as dogs shake for something that is coming to pass a long way off, knowing the horror of its vibration without exact knowledge of its location. There was not one who had not someone at the front, brother, lover, husband. It was almost impossible to get a doctor, food was said to be guarded against hoarders, matches were giving out, and maids, left in charge of their mistresses' empty houses, stood without hope at the darkened windows" ("War in Paris" 266). Barnes insists on the presence of women during wartime: suffering and terror-stricken, women continue to manage the domestic economy, even with virtually no resources. As a result, Barnes legitimizes her knowledge of and perspective on war, a move that has been traditionally foreclosed in literary accounts and war memoirs. Expounding upon the gender divide during wartime in a memorable illustration, Barnes paints a picture of hundreds and hundreds of cars in grid-locked traffic: women in cars driving away from Paris and the threat of immediate war and men in cars heading to Paris and war (267). Life on the home front in the prelude to war is validated by Barnes's personal, albeit limited, witnessing of it, which lends credibility to her gendered account of what war entails for women.

She continues her explanation of life on the home front in the following excerpt from her partially completed war memoir. This passage follows a brief comment on war's perversities: "Certainly it [fear of death] is maladjustment, but why should a man be adjusted to horror, evil, war, and death? So, though, none of us caught in Paris had seen one dead body, or heard many guns, or suffered any personal attack, neither imprisonment nor loss of men, still the fear was there, and the nerves giving away" ("War in Paris" 268). Barnes emphasizes war as an unnatural business, entrenched in "evil" and exacting death, through her string of associated perversions to which people attempt to become adjusted: "horror, evil, war, and death." She acknowledges that neither she nor her fellow female civilians have seen war battles, and yet the sheer fear of war's effects unnerves Barnes to the point of breakdowns. This observation (people should not be adjusting to what is damaging) and acknowledgment (women on the home front/living in occupied Paris suffer from war too) underscore the activity and effects of war as unnatural and perverse. The topics named in the passage also highlight the themes of emotional suffering, mental instability, and fear in *Nightwood*, all of which mirror states in which Barnes found herself in 1939 while living in Paris.

War is repeatedly referenced in treatments of the othered, feminized characters in *Nightwood*, but trends in criticism on the novel have yet to embrace it fully as a sophisticated war novel or a novel treating war as subtext, with few exceptions.[3] This chapter presents the first comprehensive study of *Nightwood* as a gendered response to trauma, namely the trauma induced by World War I and contextualized by the identity politics in the years between the two world wars.

Nightwood thus critiques war through its treatment of lives in the shadows of two world wars. But Margaret Bockting surmises that Barnes's contributions have been excluded from "the war/feminism issue" because of the "sense that her concerns were more personal and private than political" (23). This prejudice resonates with that of sentimental bias: because Barnes locates war's effects and trauma within the confines of personal female relationships and memories of war recounted by a feminized subject and couched in female models, her work is dismissed as "personal and private" and therefore not "political." Such a judgment bespeaks ingrained and long-standing bias toward the female (war) writer and leaves no space for acceptance of works that contain traces of sentimentalism or have a woman-centered perspective. Certainly, *Nightwood* does not mimic the style of sentimentalism; its difficult surrealistic style positions it firmly within the modernist movement, and yet there are sentimental aspects present in *Nightwood*. The writer Emily Coleman commented about the novel in her diary in 1932: "Most of the book is sentimental shit of the worst kind (Thelma and Fitzie), then these wonderful truths" (qtd. in Barnes, *Nightwood* viii). Nevertheless, *Nightwood* makes the personal and private political, albeit in an avant-garde surrealistic manner, in much the same way that H.D.'s *Trilogy* does.

Nightwood is not only a novel about war and trauma; it also deals with exclusionary, patriarchal politics. Gender roles are attributed to a phallogocentric discourse community within the novel, and Barnes rejects essentialist gender roles, alternatively recognizing gendered behavior as performative. The performative aspects of sexual roles and gendered behavior undermine essentialism as a valid ideological platform in *Nightwood* because Barnes underscores the arbitrary distinctions inherent in gender roles. She refutes conventional ideas of sexuality and what it means to be a man or a woman. Instead, Barnes introduces main characters, lesbians and a transvestite, who function as commentators on war and trauma through interpersonal relationships. War serves as the extended metaphor for trauma and perversity within the novel. I argue that the purported perverse story of deviant characters engaging in deviant behavior places in relief the actual perversity and corruption of its subtext: war. My objective in examining Barnes's *Nightwood* is to undertake an analysis and evaluation of female corporeality in connection with depictions of and responses to trauma in order to "represent women's bodies from points of views and interests relevant to women themselves," as Elizabeth Grosz advocates (14). Rather than engage in an essentialist examination, I will instead focus on how female corporeality and identity are represented and accessed by male and female characters and subjects in connection to war. Ultimately, war is construed as dangerous and perverse by the main characters in the novel.

I offer two detailed examples concerning how war is construed as perverse in *Nightwood* through the perspective of feminized male subjects.[4] (I discuss O'Connor's femininity in section 3.) In both examples O'Connor casts war as a perversion of civilization when narrating his war experiences. In the first example O'Connor claims to have resigned himself to his absurd lot as a soldier and explains that he donned a shroud as a result. The other soldiers are appalled at what seems to them a blatant death wish. O'Connor remembers his entry into his regiment: "And out I walked, and would you have seen this regiment! and me perfectly happy smiling over the top of it, like a bird over a hedge. They said, Holy Mother of Mercy! its [*sic*] a shroud you've put on—and the luck of that is too awful to mention!" (270). By putting on a shroud, O'Connor foregrounds the actual objective of battle: injury. He showcases the actual business of war in wearing the shroud and in the process alarms the other soldiers. Yet the unnaturalness of his situation overwhelms him. Unable to fight, O'Connor sits down and cries, with bullets whizzing by him. As he fails in his duties as a soldier, he witnesses the death of a friend; his friend's throat is ripped through by bullets. To illustrate the perversity of war further, O'Connor's fellow infantryman lies in a grotesque position after being killed—almost lifelike but not quite. After being shot in the throat, he falls into a sitting position on a tree stump, but his head is thrown back too far, and thus a natural sitting position is only mimicked. It is at this point that O'Connor loses his shroud. Once war marks itself on another's body, O'Connor no longer needs the shroud to protest the war. In relating his painful war experiences, O'Connor creates a record that indicates and speaks to a feminized body in pain as a result of war.

The second example that positions war as perverse and casts a feminized body in battle involves MacClusky, an effeminate dandy who serves in the same regiment as O'Connor. Barnes makes it clear that MacClusky, the sensitive performer who could act "the dying swan," has no place in the masculine-coded project of war: he is there because "people got the idea that it would be nice to shoot the world up and take the starch out of a generation." In his previous life MacClusky enjoys success as an artist performing femininity; smelling like a gardenia, he engages in lyrical dance ("the dying swan") and circus acrobatics, leaping through hoops and "swishing into the air" (275). Sharing a homosexual identity and a repulsion for the actual work of war, MacClusky finds himself as out of place on the frontlines as O'Connor. Their sex does not translate automatically into masculine-coded behavior. Yet, while O'Connor is treated as a feminine character because he cannot actively participate in war, MacClusky succeeds in an ironic performance of masculinity. His performance is ironic in that he is celebrated as a soldier for his unpredictable feminine response in battle, behavior that ensures an advantage against the enemy:

> He'd been standing in the middle of a bridge trying to think where the war was coming from when a douse of Germans loomed up, trying to make the bridge before MacClusky found out, and there he was, the poor frail, gone wild in the center of the pontoon, and instead of shooting—and why should he know one end of a gun from another—he just went all of a fluff, if you can call murder fluff, and swung the heft around and began banging their heads off, and they flew like crazy because even a war has certain calculable reactive processes and this wasn't one of them, so off they flew, seeing what

> they thought was a wild man in their midst who had no respect whatsoever for the correct forms of slaughter. So he held the fort, as it were, swinging away with the butt of that thing. (276)

Although male, MacClusky—"the poor frail"—is completely unfit for masculine war business as the business is usually executed. Inexpert and even clueless about weapons, he represents both a feminized and masculine body in war. MacClusky enacts male and female performances: he may be effeminate, but he manages to kill a significant number of soldiers. The description "murderous fluff" perfectly captures the gendered tensions. MacClusky's reaction to war translates into "female" hysteria, and yet, while hysteric, he successfully executes the duties of a combatant. O'Connor further emphasizes MacClusky's response to the perversity of war (the unmaking of civilization) at his decoration ceremony: "And it got about, and all of us grinning because we knew it was the moment his balls fell out with misery and horror that he got the idea." MacClusky suffers textual emasculation due to an emotional display of war trauma through his feminized and queer body, but another interpretation could read *fell out* in the sense of "descended," meaning that MacClusky's genitalia is not visible until he becomes violent (in order to save his own life) in battle. Nevertheless, O'Connor thinks of MacClusky as queer and unprepared, even naive, as a result of the excessive emotional display: "I've never seen any tears like those before in my life, though that is the way a boy cries who has been queer all of his hour" (277).

MacClusky may be portrayed as queer, feminine, and naive, but he proves to be a successful solider. In this illustration Barnes collapses the gendered tensions in war between male active roles and female passive roles in wartime by blurring the line between acceptable and unacceptable gender performances. Significantly, she casts war as perverse in detailing MacClusky's reaction to it, specifically in the unmaking of him as civilian. MacClusky is the most unlikely candidate for battle; Barnes wants us to understand that he is cultured, feminine, and naive about what war entails. And yet war perverts MacClusky and turns him into a killer; he engages in, as Barnes notes, "murder" and "slaughter."

Punishable Identities in *Nightwood*

The abject, marginalized identities in *Nightwood* figure as subjects with bodies in pain, and the stories of these marginalized bodies create a narrative that legitimizes suffering and trauma and counters generic patriarchal war narratives. I maintain that *Nightwood* sets up contexts of war and trauma to trace the suffering of the characters and to critique the oppressive and life-threatening discourses and ideologies that force the characters to "bow down" and/or perish.[5]

In her celebrated work on *Nightwood* Jane Marcus examines the abject figures in *Nightwood* as characters who are entrenched in political resistance but who are also constituted as victims. *Nightwood* "figures by absence the authoritarian dominators of Europe in the 1930s, the sexual and political fascists" (Marcus 221). All of the marginalized characters are consigned to invisibility by mainstream society, as O'Connor's barroom accusation later in the novel attests.[6] They possess identities that are punishable in the novel.

O'Connor regularly comments upon the dangers of behaving outside of categorization. His ruminations serve as horrific "foreshadowing" and commentary: the possibility of punishment is omnipresent if one misperforms or rejects essentialist identity characteristics: "If they must punish you for forgetting yourself. . . . Why don't they come to your house in the dark, when no one is looking, and let your drawers down and beat you up?" (28). Any categorical identity designation inherently contains the ability to circumscribe and marginalize. Marginalization breeds desperation, violence, and persecution, as O'Connor insinuates: "And it's strange and awful how many people there are who can do what they want only off a roof, or through a rope, or under water, or after the shot is silent" (25). This last assertion is ambiguous; it can allude to suicide or to murder or to both acts. Political persecution can result in murder, and, when persecuted people misperform, when they "do what they want," the result may be hanging or drowning or death by a firing squad. On the other hand, O'Connor may mean that because persecuted people are relegated to the margins and sometimes forcibly controlled, the only agency or freedom such people achieve is through suicide. Even this morbid passage alludes to O'Connor's concern with performance when it plays off of his observation that "they must punish you for forgetting yourself"; to forget oneself means to misperform gender in O'Connor's case or to fall short of societal expectations for what one is supposed to be, and misperforming is dangerous because deviant behavior was criminalized in the early twentieth century.

O'Connor opens himself up to punishment by upsetting conventional distinctions relating to gendered performances when, for instance, he dresses in women's clothes and wears women's cosmetics. He becomes the representative liminal character, the disenfranchised man who identifies himself as the third sex, a woman born in a man's body. O'Connor declares, "It was more than a boy like me (who am the last woman left in this world, though I am the bearded lady) could bear" (84). In this statement he collapses the male/female binary opposition in relation to his own identity.

In terms of disqualification O'Connor's liminal identity is a liability. Meryl Altman remarks, "Essentialisms now make us justifiably suspicious, for reasons one might trace back negatively to Hitler" (162). O'Connor harbors an identity, that of a homosexual transvestite, that will become increasingly dangerous as time passes, and the text is appropriately gloomy when considering him in what should be construed as a safe haven, his home: "The room was so small that it was just possible to walk sideways up to the bed, it was as if being condemned to the grave, the doctor had decided to occupy it with the utmost abandon" (68). Nora's reaction to O'Connor in his bed emphasizes the pessimistic tone of the omniscient narrator. Discovering O'Connor in a woman's flannel nightgown with a blond wig and heavily made up, Nora is dismayed, although she too is an outsider to convention. O'Connor has completely "evacuated custom," and Nora tends to circumspection when in public; she usually avoids causing scenes and drawing attention to herself and her relationship with Robin, preferring instead to follow Robin at a distance if she follows at all. O'Connor, on the other hand, presents Nora with what she very much dislikes—a spectacle.

Spectacles are dangerous, *Nightwood* insinuates, as are unconventional behaviors.[7] Once the subject performs as spectacle, the subject becomes vulnerable, as O'Connor seems to realize when he is confronted in drag: "You see that you can ask me anything" (69). He later adds: "And what am I? I'm damned, and carefully public!" (134). From O'Connor's perspective his unsanctioned performances are carefully executed in his personal space without punishment—for the present time. But he displays an awareness of potential punishment ("And what am I? I'm damned"). Unable to avoid the spectacle once she has encountered it, Nora stays to learn about "the night"—"fear bottom-out and wrong side up" that "does something to a person's identity, even when asleep"—from O'Connor (70). In the novel *night* suggests a space of license or expanded agency. It is not synonymous with *freedom*, but "night" is the time when aberrant characters who do not conform to social, or "daytime," norms can act with more impunity. The subject of war presents itself as an ironic and perceptive subtext for those subjects (e.g., O'Connor and Nora) who will be hunted during the murderous purging of World War II.

Always insightful, O'Connor foreshadows a second world war: "No man needs curing of his individual sickness; his universal malady is what he should look to" (32). I read the "universal malady" that O'Connor refers to as global sickness in the form of war. His advice that people "should look to" it hints at persecution, but O'Connor is firm that the persecuted person (or scapegoat) is not the problem ("No man needs curing of his individual sickness"). Rather, people like O'Connor are devoid of responsibility concerning war; his deviance is not the problem. The problem is the brute extermination of difference. Marcus also points to the threat of punishment and war tensions in connection with marginal identities within *Nightwood*: "The evening of the 'living statues' and outcasts at the Count's is a museum of soon-to-be exterminated human types, like Hitler's Jewish Museum at Prague, meant to be all that was left of Jewish culture after the Holocaust" (231). Everyone (possessing an identity of alterity) is symbolically expelled from the count's party early in the novel, with Frau Mann the circus performer mournfully informing her friends, "I've an album of my own . . . and everyone in it looks like a solider—even though they are dead" (26). The threat of persecution is tied to war terms and metaphors because war symbolizes trauma and perversity (corruption).

Nightwood centers the marginal characters, following their lives and delving into their embodied states, thus making them visible. O'Connor accuses heteronormative society of rendering difference invisible: "What people! All queer in a terrible way. There were a couple of queer *good* people once in this world—but none of you . . . will ever know them. You think you are all studded with diamonds, don't you?" (133). Addressing the entire room in a crowded bar, O'Connor accuses the dominant group of being constituents in a terrible and queer (read: unnatural) collective group who will foreclose the opportunity to acquaint themselves with good queer (read: homosexual) people because of their supposedly prized ("diamond") status.

Homosexuality is not the only identity that is tied to punishment, war stories, and war metaphors. Displaced from Italy and Austria and eventually France, Felix roams from place to place, desperately clinging to his falsified family tradition and fabricated past. He belongs nowhere. Felix is the most abject and othered character in the novel, and, while his characterization does make use of circulated stereotypes, Mairéad Hanrahan argues that Felix's characterization calls essentialist Jewish identity into question because "the Barnesian Jew suffers from so total a lack of identity, so unredeemable a confusion that any attempt to redeem his condition only aggravates it"; Felix functions "only in his relationship to the Other, his relationship *as* Other, so Other than even his Otherness does not belong to him" (32). I bring Felix into my discussion of *Nightwood* because his alterity complements the positions of the main characters. His liminal and marginal identity mirrors the somewhat precarious positions that O'Connor, Nora, and Robin occupy. Each character possesses an identity that is deviant and therefore punishable by the dominant society.

Within the text Felix is described as hunting for the evidence of his "disqualification" (9). I concur with Cheryl Plumb's definition of Barnes's use of *disqualification:* "She seems to refer to an awareness of a sense of shame, a suggestion that individuals who incurred public dismissal or scrutiny suffered because of what had happened to them or what they were, that is, Jewish, homosexual, or alienated from the values of the dominant culture" ("Introduction" xviii). I will add that, in my reading of *Nightwood,* disqualification also applies to the sense of fear or endangerment that marginalized characters feel toward potentially traumatic events that can happen to them in the future as a result of assuming an identity of alterity. Disqualification passes down along ethnic and gendered lines in *Nightwood.* In terms of gendered behavior and expectations, for instance, when he talks about misperforming and punishment, O'Connor expresses fears concerning disqualification.

Felix already possesses an artifact of his disqualification; his yellow and black handkerchief marks him textually as a Jew, although no one else can read the significance of the ancestral handkerchief that harks back to medieval Roman circuses in which Jews were forced to run like animals and become spectacles. This animal reference ascribes femininity to Felix; in all other instances in the novel animals are associated with female war trauma and marginalization. Hanrahan elaborates on the significance of the handkerchief to the construction of Jewish identity in the text, with special attention paid to marginalization and the threat of punishment: "The colours of the handkerchief are the yellow and black into which primordial chaos was first differentiated; yellow is also the colour of the Star of David, with which Nazis were beginning to mark out the Jews at the time of writing *Nightwood*. In Guido's gesture [wiping his tears on the marked handkerchief] can be read the desire to preserve the memory of a singular event by which his people were set apart, circumscribed, a symbolic circumcision of the race rather than of the individual" (36). The sinister and chilling implications of Felix's and his son Guido's disqualification reverberate through the text due to its cultural context, whether or not Barnes intentionally developed this treatment. Marcus remarks on the resonance of the handkerchief and the medieval circuses "in which outcast Jews were terrorized": the handkerchief and mention of medieval circuses in *Nightwood* "prophesy with chilling accuracy the Nazi destruction of millions of Jews and other outcasts, devoured by their modern technological lions, the gas chambers and ovens of the concentration camps" (239–40). Moreover, the handkerchief speaks to the historical victimization of the Jew, and the circus represents a place where marginal people can congregate: Robin and Nora meet for the first time at a circus. Barnes shapes the circus as a sphere open to the disqualified, including Felix, who, although not homosexual, feels most at home with his disenfranchised and socially unacceptable circus friends. Julie Abraham suggests that, by taking on the experience of the excluded, Barnes could "situate her own work relative to the official record, circumventing the initial fact of her subjects' historical and, by extension, literary disqualification" (255). I would complicate and elaborate upon Abraham's view by suggesting in what way Barnes writes around (and about) historical and literary disqualification: she foregrounds the very trauma and exclusionary politics embedded in the conditions of marginalization.

For the most part feminized and homosexual bodies are outside the phallogocentric system of acknowledgment and validation: "'And do I know my Sodomites?' the doctor said unhappily, 'and what the heart goes bang up against if it loves one of them, especially if it's a woman loving one of them. What do they find then, that this lover has committed the unpardonable error of not being able to exist'" (79). The homosexual community that O'Connor refers to in this passage is rendered invisible. Heterosexual practices and patriarchal Logos foster estrangement for the lesbian and the male homosexual transvestite; these subjects resort to working and living outside of the dominant system. O'Connor remarks, "The Bible lies the one way, but the night gown the other" (70). Metaphorically, O'Connor gives the Bible as an example of a text encompassing Logos on one end of the spectrum and the nightgown as a sign of performative perversity in diametric opposition. Living and working outside of the dominant system opens marginalized subjects up to punishment and disenfranchisement. They are labeled perverse because they do not conform to the dominant society's sanctioned performances and expectations; thus, such marginalized figures have limited agency to effect change and suffer circumscribed visibility within society.

The circumscription of a lesbian identity presented a political problem for Barnes, from her perspective, in terms of her literary reputation and personal life. She suspected that her reputation as a lesbian marginalized her and her work. Throughout her life Barnes maintained in documents and conversations that the notion she was a lesbian "was nonsense" (O'Neal 25). In fact, Barnes was adamant in her protestations late in her life that she was heterosexual and even became angered at professions of admiration by members of the lesbian community. Barnes railed against a small bookstore named after her, thinking it must be a lesbian-themed bookstore: "She is outraged by its existence," recorded Hank O'Neal. "How dare they," Barnes purportedly fumed, "it is probably a terrible little lesbian bookshop" (19). O'Neal's account of his friendship with Barnes overflows with her denunciation of lesbianism—particularly when she is categorically concerned with questions of lesbian identity and marginalization:

> In her mind there was a distinct stigma attached to being a lesbian, and her association with lesbianism weighed heavily on her: she thought it had tainted her reputation. . . . Once when I returned from a lengthy business trip, Barnes said I'd stayed away so long because one of our mutual friends had told me Miss Barnes was a lesbian. I wondered whether the publication of *Nightwood*, the attendant "widespread" belief that she was a lesbian, and the apparent social disgraces she felt caused her withdrawal into a nearly monastic existence. It seemed absurd, particularly after considering her lifestyle of the previous twenty-five years, but she made so much of how it had changed her life that in my mind it became a strong possibility. (172)

Barnes's repudiation of an identity so readily ascribed to her seems puzzling from the outset when her biography and past relationships suggest otherwise. On the one hand, Barnes appears to have been bisexual, and she may have resented being labeled and pinned to a single sexual identity when her own sexuality could not be clearly or cleanly categorized.[8] On the other hand, Barnes may have grown increasingly conservative and crotchety, perhaps delighting in turning away her lesbian admirers, as O'Neal suggests in his memoir.

Another possibility may be that she simply felt it was too much of a burden to be a champion for lesbianism after the notoriety she received for *Nightwood;* she often wondered how she had written the novel and reflected that she would never be able to write another masterpiece like it. As Erin Carlston remarks, noting the exception of Sappho, "Women writers living and writing a sexuality that had rarely been represented in any literature not explicitly pornographic were bound to look to men's writings to ground their own sexual and textual histories" (49). It is therefore more than likely, given her attitude in the earlier passage by O'Neal, that Barnes may have rejected the categorization of *Nightwood* as a lesbian novel in part because she feared marginalization as an author of a lesbian work. As Barnes insinuates to O'Neal through her talk of stigmatization, she believed that being classified as a lesbian reduced her worth as a person and rendered her work less appealing to a heterosexual audience. She seemed to find, at least late in her life, that her purported lesbian identity was punishable in the form of diminishing interest in her and her work.

O'Connor as Feminized Subject and Professor of Trauma

Victimized by war, O'Connor repeatedly talks out his trauma in feminized ways, thereby rejecting the silence imposed on female war trauma. Referring to himself and Marie Antoinette as "the two blasphemed queens," O'Connor compares rows of silk dresses to soldiers going off to war: "There was enough spirit in those old materials to get shot" (26). Constantly thinking about war and gender, O'Connor reflects on the sexual politics and traumas he has known and integrates insights and examples from his past experiences for his audience.

O'Connor forges a relationship between war and his feminized body explicitly: "'You see before you, madame,' he said, 'one who, in common parlance is called a 'faggot,' a 'fairy,' a 'queen.' I was created in anxiety. My father, Lord rest his soul, had no happiness of me from the beginning. When I joined the army he relented a little because he had a suspicion that possibly in that fracas which occasionally puts a son on the list of 'not much since,' I might be damaged. . . . For a moment he seemed to realize my terrible predicament: to be shot for man's meat, but to go down like a girl, crying in the night for her mother" (64–65). The binary structures inherent in war underpin O'Connor's and his father's understanding of war as male/active business rather than female/passive activity. His father suspects that his son will be damaged in the war because his feminine behavior consigns him to the subject position of passive victim ("man's meat"), which will deny him full, active participation in the war as a male soldier. O'Connor and his father assign a female, passive response to his hypothetical war participation ("crying in the night for her mother") because of his femininity. But O'Connor participates in battle and is thus given an opportunity to express pain as a victim occupying a feminized body.

To prove his manhood, O'Connor enlists in the army to perform masculinity, but he resents both the results of the performance and what it entails. According to O'Connor, "I gave my kidney on the left side to France in the war. . . . I've drunk myself half around the world cursing her [France] for jerking it [the kidney] out—if I had it to do again, grand country though it is—I'd be the girl found lurking behind the army, or up with the hill folk" (77). Margaret Bockting reads this passage as Barnes drawing attention "to the value of disillusionment with the binary constructions of gender that helped to sustain war" (32). What I find significant in O'Connor's confession is his preference for feminine behavior ("I'd be the girl found lurking behind the army"), and the depiction of him suffering emotionally ("drunk myself half around the world cursing [France]") and physically ("jerking [the kidney] out"). O'Connor legitimizes a kind of female suffering in his authorized account as a gender-bending soldier. Barnes does not deliver verbalized accounts of war and suffering from Robin, Nora, or Jenny; the women of *Nightwood* are unable to articulate their responses to war and suffering except through substitutes—and O'Connor comes closest to being a woman without actually being one. And yet O'Connor is construed in very different ways than Robin. He is depicted as traumatized but healing (he is able to talk out his trauma), probably because he was an acknowledged participant in war and is biologically male. As a combat veteran, his suffering receives heterosexual and patriarchal approbation. In fact, he enlists in the army in order to receive that very approbation from his father, who intuits his son is queer. Conversely, Robin endures trauma passively and is unable to voice her pain until her complete breakdown at the very end of the novel, and, even then, her pain is vocalized through barking and crying, sounds that do not coherently signify in the text. Robin's body is disqualified from phallogocentric approbation as a female homosexual who experiences war trauma. As a result, O'Connor is the only character who can tell stories about war.

O'Connor occupies both male and female subject positions in spite of the fact that in descriptions his body is usually feminized. He is the only character who can "pass" back and forth between male and female identities. He possesses extra authority to tell war stories because of his veteran status, and at the same time he can critique the phallogocentrism of war and the world in general. As both a man and a feminine subject, O'Connor is perhaps the best teacher of trauma and war because his instruction is not confined by and does not conform to societal expectations of gender. I contend that O'Connor's stories are meant to teach Nora; they consist of O'Connor's reflections on trauma, and Nora is expected to extrapolate insight and lessons from O'Connor's experiences because she lacks her own stories or at least access to other women's stories. Nora's psychological and emotional trauma is figured in embodied language, but, before meeting O'Connor, she is oblivious to the nature of trauma. She has not reflected on it, and O'Connor has to explain her situation to her: "There is a gap in 'world pain' through which the singular falls continually and forever; a body falling in observable space, deprived of the privacy of disappearance; as if privacy, moving relentlessly away, by the very sustaining power of its withdrawal kept the body eternally moving downward; but in one place, and perpetually before the eye. Such a singular was Nora. There was some derangement in her equilibrium that kept her immune to her own descent" (47). With the end of "privacy" in connection with her trauma, resulting in O'Connor's gaze fixed upon her, Nora will become self-aware. He serves as both her confidant and teacher in regard to pain and suffering. Unable to depict Nora in direct contact with war, Barnes resorts to using O'Connor as the figure—through his authority as a soldier, a physician, and a man—who teaches Nora about war and trauma. Nora, then, is taught by a man who configures himself as a woman. This indistinctness has important consequences for the representation of war and trauma: there is space for men and women (and ambiguity) in narratives and treatments of war.

O'Connor relates a series of war stories in *Nightwood*, and his stories are meant to communicate something about the gendering of experience in wartime, with implications for Nora or another addressee. In his first war story O'Connor uses the cow as a metaphor for human war experience. The cow story, similar to O'Connor's other narratives, is relatively brief: in absolute terror of the bombardment, the cow urinates and excretes upon her own body without any apparent control and sheds tears (19–20). Nora is the recipient of this particular story, and O'Connor, as her self-appointed teacher, relates it to her in order to instruct her on the nature of trauma: trauma is an embodied experience, as the cow story illustrates. The female body of the cow speaks its trauma through the excessive flow of bodily waste and tears. The cow's suffering registers, but its manifestation is almost incomprehensible or unreadable as female responses to trauma always are in *Nightwood*. O'Connor cryptically avers, "I thought, there are directions and speeds that no one has calculated, for believe it or not that cow had gone somewhere very fast that we didn't know of, and yet was still standing there" (20). The cow's suffering is unfathomable ("the cow had gone somewhere very fast that we didn't know of") in its extraliterary state: the cow's trauma is outside of verbal language and representation. Indeed, the cow's body is utterly abject; bodily fluids and matter are flowing freely, and this condition further condemns the cow's body as something that should not be represented in intelligible discourse.

The cow story illustrates the problem Barnes, H.D., and Stein came up against in their literary work: how can a female civilian best represent female trauma and bodies in literature treating war when female bodies and suffering have traditionally been rendered invisible in war narrative? Barnes resorts to cryptic and perverse (deviant) treatments that correlate to the truly perverse (corrupt) exclusionary treatment of women's bodies in relation to war. With no models to follow in the form of modernist war novels written by American women, Barnes employs intimations, suggestions, and indirect representations of female bodies in pain, often likening the bodies to animals as a nod to the lack of opportunity for female bodies to signify in texts meaningfully.

O'Connor erodes expectations concerning gender and war in his lessons on trauma. Recalling the war, for instance, he tells Nora another story: "'I was in a war once myself,' the doctor went on, 'in a little town where the bombs began tearing the heart out of you, so that you began to think of all the majesty in the world that you would not be able to think of in a minute if the noise came down and struck in the right place" (19). Emphasizing the emotional and psychological terror of war, O'Connor the soldier privileges a sentimental, feminized experience of war rather than a masculine show of heroic bravery. Instead of performing to essentialist expectations, O'Connor's description is sentimental in its emotional tone and intimacy; he invites Nora to identify with him through his use of second-person pronouns and through his insinuation that she is a veteran too. ("I was in a war once myself" implies that Nora is currently in the midst of a war or has war experience.) Also, O'Connor's word choices denote an emotional involvement ("the bombs began tearing the *heart* out of you"). By acknowledging an emotional response that invites female identification on the part of Nora, he begins the work of validating female presence in connection with war and war narrative.

The stories that O'Connor shares with Nora anticipate her psychoanalytic confiding in him. Nora's trauma takes the form of desperate codependency on Robin: she informs O'Connor that every hour is her last, and "one can't live one's last hour all one's life!" (113). Her suffering is treated sympathetically by O'Connor. He expresses pity for her when he declares, "You never loved anyone before, and you'll never love anyone again, as you love Robin" (114). Nora insists on verbalizing this loss to O'Connor, and he continues to instruct her through war examples and figures of speech invoking war. When Nora asks what will happen to her and to Robin, he tells her, "My war has brought me many things; let yours bring you as much" (109). O'Connor teaches Nora about trauma through comparisons of her domestic experience to his veteran experience. The stories he relates for Nora's enlightenment reference both his own literal war memories and, metaphorically, Nora's war with the war-damaged Robin. Because he retains the framework of war in discussing his and Nora's trauma, he alludes to the possibility of war-related female suffering when he assumes that Nora will be able to understand what she is meant to extrapolate from his lessons. Because Robin has been affected by something catastrophic, presumably an incident or incidents related to World War I, Nora may well be able to sift through O'Connor's war stories and lessons on trauma to develop insight into her relationship with Robin.

Trauma and Proxies: O'Connor's Animal Stories and Nora and Robin's Doll Baby

When giving advice to Felix and Nora about Robin, O'Connor resorts to war stories, invoking a traumatized horse in his lesson for Felix and a dead horse in his lesson for Nora. Alan Singer interprets O'Connor's use of war imagery, specifically in relation to the horse, as metaphoric analogies that preclude meaning for Felix and Nora, probably because they either lack knowledge of war rhetoric or cannot talk about war or trauma in an accessible or articulate manner. I interpret the horse as a war symbol that functions as a literal reference to O'Connor's war knowledge and as a metaphor that compares his war experience to the trauma of Robin and that of her lovers. I disagree with Singer's assertion that the characters cannot understand O'Connor's metaphoric analogies because "the metaphor of the horse is a point of departure rather than a reservoir of accumulated meanings" (65). The horse symbol is not irrelevant or a point of departure because the animal imagery crops up again in relation to Robin at the end of the novel, and O'Connor tells two different horse stories to two different people. As such, I maintain that the horse is indeed a "reservoir of accumulated meanings." The story of the horse is meant to teach a lesson; the addressee is supposed to extrapolate meaning. Although Felix and Nora did not participate in the frontlines of World War I, they both lived through it on the home front, and they would be familiar with key conceptual categories and cultural signifiers put into place by it. According to Paul Fussell, "Even if . . . attenuated and largely metaphorical, the diction of war resides everywhere just below the surface of modern experience. . . . One is recalling war and yet with a sense that such figures are somehow most appropriate to the modern situation" (189). Even with the cessation of World War I, war diction and stories surface in O'Connor's speech, betraying the indelible imprint of war on him. War has culturally marked Nora too, for she is able to understand O'Connor.

The problematic situation of representing female wartime trauma is underscored in O'Connor's horse stories. The horse featured in O'Connor's war story, as told to Felix, is sexed and gendered as female, and it is depicted as physically and psychologically mourning the death of its colt. O'Connor relates the story of "the horse who knew too much" to Felix: "Take the case of the horse who knew too much. . . . She was in mourning for something taken away from her in a bombardment in the war—by the way she stood, that something lay between her hooves—she stirred no branch though her hide was a river of sorrow; she was damned to her hocks" (96). Barnes explains that in this scene the horse, "in the shock of war, gave premature birth" (226). Mourning the loss of her colt and suffering due to war activity, the horse's body speaks her pain: the emphasis in this illustration is on female, animalized corporeality. The horse's embodied state protests her war knowledge, and Barnes fleshes out the horse's situation in embodied language: her stance and her hide belie her loss, and the loss is construed as a corporeal loss in the body of the colt. The bombardment causes the horse actively to suffer as emphasized through her stillborn delivery, and her feminized body is "damned" by war. As with O'Connor's other war stories, Felix is supposed to extract meaning from O'Connor's war experience and apply what he has learned to his own noncombatant life. The crucial insights into war, couched in animalistic and feminine images, are presented by a veteran to another man.

Barnes is unable fully to assign women the voices they need to articulate war and trauma, but we may read the proxies in *Nightwood* as evidence that female presence can be hinted at and alluded to. While I do read the horse's body as speaking to dangers encroaching upon human female bodies, the body illustrated is still that of a horse. Perhaps because Barnes did not serve in the war effort, she is unable to interpellate women into war narrative as fully as H.D. and Stein, who both served as war relief workers. Barnes seems incapable of casting human female characters and depicting their bodies explicitly in positions related to war. Instead, she traces female war trauma and marks female presence in war narrative in an indirect manner, treating the effects of war on female bodies through animal references and stories.

O'Connor continues to draw upon war imagery when speaking to Nora. Although Nora is a noncombatant, O'Connor presumes she will not only understand but will profit from his tale. In his next war story, featuring an unsexed horse, O'Connor narrates: "Once in the war I saw a dead horse that had been lying long against the ground. Time and the birds, and its own last concentration had removed the body a great way from the head. As I looked upon that head, my memory weighed for the lost body; and because of that missing quantity even heavier hung that head along the ground. So love, when it has gone, taking time with it, leaves a memory of its weight" (107–8). Again, O'Connor's story is firmly grounded in corporeal imagery and victimization. The horse could conceivably be assigned either a male or female identity, but Barnes genders the horse as female in the other war story she assigns to O'Connor. Likewise, possessing a body that he characterizes and often performs as feminine, O'Connor notably empathizes with the body of the horse, thus superimposing his feminized body ("As I looked upon that head, my memory weighed for the lost body") onto the unsexed horse and perhaps feminizing it in the process. On the other hand, O'Connor's unique position of occupying both male and female attributes suggests that the sex of the horse may not matter; the horse can serve as a substitute for a male or female victim. What is clear is O'Connor's identification with the horse: O'Connor's memory strangely transforms into the dead horse's memory, creating a shared experience between the dead horse and the trauma of his own war experience. The decapitated body, like the previous horse's body, speaks its trauma through its graphic (i.e., represented) dismemberment.

Notably, here O'Connor juxtaposes his war experience with female suffering; Nora is supposed to be able to identify with the story about a dead horse, suggesting that the horse as participant/casualty might be meaningful to female experience. Specifically, Robin serves as the focal point at which O'Connor's layers of meaning in the story intersect or converge: damaged by war memories (like O'Connor), as the novel insinuates, Robin causes Nora unmitigated grief as the love that "has gone" and "leaves a memory of its weight." Addressed to Nora by O'Connor, with Robin as its subject, this story invokes three feminized, suffering bodies (O'Connor, Nora, and Robin/the "lost body" of the horse), and the corporeal language insists on their trauma and physical presence. The confusion and blurring of gender boundaries promotes and conflates the equalizing of men and women in war narrative. One effect of this conflation results in the metaphoric components of a male vehicle (O'Connor the authoritative storyteller) and a female tenor (war ravages involving feminized subjects and female trauma).

Another representation of female suffering in *Nightwood* is the abused doll baby. The extent to which Robin is afflicted is illustrated in her treatment of the doll she gives Nora. Originally, the doll was meant as a gift from Robin to Nora as a token of their love; it is a substitute for the child that could be produced in a heterosexual relationship. The doll signifies the traumatic end/death of the lesbian relationship of Nora and Robin after Robin crushes it. Robin is too scarred and unhealthy to participate in a healthy relationship and destroys her "offspring" in the process. Helpless, the doll becomes a feminized casualty. Again, we have a representative of a traumatized female subject that is not human. O'Connor's two horse stories and his cow story share with Robin and Nora's inanimate doll the status of proxy. The doll (and the horses and the cow) speak trauma through their brutalized and traumatized bodies for the women of *Nightwood*. As a nod to the seriousness of the incident, Barnes kept the broken doll, given to her by her former girlfriend Thelma Wood, for the rest of her life (Field 168).

As a witness to Robin's cruelty to their doll baby, Nora begins to read her relationship with Robin as traumatizing. While the doll baby could have functioned as a sacred relic of their love, it works as a broken reminder of the unhealthiness, the dis-ease (correlating to Robin's sickness as shell-shocked *somnambule*), of their relationship. Although Barnes is unable or refuses to represent female bodies fully as participants in war, the inanimate doll, like the animals, functions as a substitute for traumatized female subjects and female bodies in pain.

The Shell-Shocked Female Civilian

Nightwood is not a roman à clef, but Barnes culled material from her world and experience to re-create the surrealistic nightmarish world of *Nightwood*. In her September 20, 1935, letter to Emily Coleman, Barnes admits that "a great deal of my writing is intuition, remembrance of time and pain" (qtd. in Plumb, "Revising" 153–54). The characters derive from actual models, people Barnes knew, but the derivations take liberties and sometimes combine models/people to form a single character. In Barnes criticism, for example, Robin is universally acknowledged to be a thinly veiled Thelma Wood (American sculptor, 1901–70), Barnes's well-known lover from her Left Bank years.[9] Barnes herself admits in letters to friends that her relationship with Thelma informs her portrayal of Robin. Indeed, a purported lover of Wood's accused Barnes of driving Wood to suicidal thoughts: "Your book has ruined Thelma's life, she is deadly ill & threatening suicide because of it." Wood physically retaliated when Barnes would read *Nightwood* aloud: she hit Barnes in the mouth, knocked her down twice, and threw a cup of tea at her (Herring 165). And yet there appears to be another life model who informed the characterization of Robin, making Robin a composite character. (This doubling of Robin in the text is meaningful in the blurring and affirmation of multiple subject positions.) In his persuasive essay Lynn DeVore posits that the dada artist Baroness Elsa von

Freytag-Loringhoven (1875–1927), known as "the Baroness," served as a model for Robin.[10] DeVore is the first Barnes critic who persuasively charts the importance of the Baroness to Barnes and expounds upon the similarities between her life and Robin's fictionalized portrayal.[11] This connection between von Freytag-Loringhoven and Robin is critical in establishing Robin as a victim of war-related trauma.

The relationship with the Baroness scarred Barnes, who discussed her with O'Neal more than fifty years after her death, apparently feeling a sense of responsibility toward her and her work. The Baroness emerges as a very emotionally damaged person in her correspondence with Barnes, which positions her as the perfect real-life model and counterpart for Robin. As Barnes knew, once von Freytag-Loringhoven had landed in postwar Germany in the mid-1920s, depression, panic attacks, and suicidal tendencies plagued her; the Baroness was also generally afraid and alone (DeVore 77). In December 1924 Barnes describes her as a "citizen of terror, a contemporary without a country" (qtd. in Gammel 350).

If Robin is modeled after von Freytag-Loringhoven, as I strongly suspect and contend that she is, then the Baroness's experience of the aftermath of World War I and her subsequent traumas take on intertextual dimensions when coupled with Robin's bizarre behavior, allowing the Baroness's lived experience as expressed in her letters to Barnes to inform and correspond to the psychology and behavior of the most "lost" character in the novel, the traumatized Robin Vote. In a letter to Barnes the Baroness confessed: "I fight brave as I am and always was, but brave ones fall in war. I am not truly deranged even, but scattered—muted by fear, picking bits of heart flesh with its relentless beak, day and night, minute by minute, I must succumb soon" (27–28). The Baroness even used a war metaphor to represent her trauma to Barnes. War, then, becomes the larger-than-life trauma that overshadows Robin's life and may explain some of her seemingly shell-shocked behavior.

The most significant similarity between Robin and the Baroness is the characterization of them both as somnambulist.[12] Robin has an entire chapter dedicated to her under this name, and the Baroness describes herself as a "somnambule" in her autobiography (of which Barnes gained possession) and in one of the letters to Barnes from Germany: "I am somnambule—

shaken to awakeness before abyss of absolute icy nonsense—*as far as I am concerned*!" (23). My understanding of Robin hinges upon decoding the cause of her traumatized state, which I liken to the condition of sleepwalking. Drawing a connection between Robin and the Baroness thus becomes key in associating Robin with war terror. Indeed, sleepwalking is the only medical condition with which she is diagnosed in *Nightwood*, and so it may provide a clue to her traumatized state. Comparisons to the Baroness aside, I maintain that Robin's sleepwalking tendencies are really the vehicle, or metaphor, for her war trauma. Both sleepwalking and shell shock involve the subconscious mind and unresolved issues and problems; both conditions result in illogical and abnormal behavior. Additionally, there is a measure of uncertainty in what will happen next to someone sleepwalking or acutely suffering. Yet perhaps most striking is the degree of unrest and dis-ease that becomes readily apparent in the descriptions of Robin as comatose sleepwalker in the chapter "La Somnambule" and as hysteric in the last chapter, "The Possessed."

Shell shock emerged as a condition induced by World War I trauma, involving soldiers who experienced emotional and psychological breakdowns. Ruth Leys defines shell shock as hysteria—male hysteria—accompanied by psychological wounds rather than physical lesions (83). Borrowing a disease associated with male war combatants, Barnes superimposes it on her female character who has survived World War I and exhibits symptoms of shell shock, war-related trauma, and hysteria. To reiterate, the novel ends with Robin succumbing to a hysteric outburst and experiencing a psychological and emotional breakdown, complete with barking and tears, while battling a dog. She is unable to resolve her pain throughout the novel, and O'Connor, not a licensed physician, diagnoses her simply with sleepwalking. Her war trauma does not even register to him in the text as anything other than that.

As a result, Robin is increasingly depicted throughout *Nightwood* in animalistic terms because she is disqualified as a subject from receiving qualified help: instead of a licensed doctor practiced in war trauma or shell shock, a falsely credentialed gynecologist attends to her illness. Instead of showing empathy or sympathy toward Robin, Nora blames Robin for traumatizing *her*. On all counts Robin is successfully marginalized by her trauma, and Barnes prevents Robin from having a voice in *Nightwood;* she is forbidden from speaking out her trauma or receiving much-needed attention and help. As such, Robin self-medicates through drinking binges and promiscuity. The acknowledgment she so desperately needs is foreclosed, and she resorts to battling with Nora's dog in the chapter "The Possessed." The novel closes with Robin relinquishing her human subjectivity and performing bestial behavior instead; possessed by trauma, she becomes bestial and "barks" her pain, which resonates as a textual cry of protest. In *Nightwood* there is something extralinguistic about trauma; female trauma does not register or signify clearly but is figured, instead, as animalized and sometimes indecipherable. Representations of female trauma or war experience cannot be accessed overtly or discussed directly, as we have seen with O'Connor's animal stories.

Like Robin, the Baroness suffered from the effects of disqualification and was, in fact, marginalized because of her difference: "Tragedy is written on me—stigmatizing me—people, dull as they are, perceive it—they are never *too dull* to disapprove of something different from themselves—also to fear it or—if down—stone it—or pity it—" ("Selections" 29). Irene Gammel argues in her comprehensive and impressive biography of the Baroness that

> the Baroness's body of terror was pivotal during the World War I era. Written on her body was the trauma of earlier experiences including the tension of perpetual conflict and emotional violence at home. The Baroness's personal history had marked her body with trauma that remained largely unassimilated in her speedy journey through Europe. Memory was deeply registered on her body to be acted out during a time of collective trauma. In the midst of youthful America, by 1917 the Baroness came to represent Old Europe, associated with old age, decadence, and destruction. For America and its young modernist poets and authors . . . her body was the unsettling body of Europe at war. . . . For the exiled Europeans the reality of war they had escaped was always close by. For Americans, the memory of Old Europe was inscribed on [the Baroness's] flesh and used to terrorize a young generation of artists. (207)

The Baroness's contemporaries read her body as an accumulation of World War I–influenced signifiers that surfaced terror, trauma, and destruction. Gammel gives an additional example of the contemporary understanding of the Baroness's body as a battlefield in Theresa Bernstein's 1917 oil depiction of von Freytag-Loringhoven: a dark and thick brushstroke accentuates the entire outline of her body, which Gammel interprets as "the dark shadow of traumatic memory inscribed on the body itself" (206–7). The Baroness's body is associated with war and the aftermath of war, and we should consider Robin's sick body, a body likely modeled after the Baroness's own, to be war ravaged as well.

Barnes's relationship with von Freytag-Loringhoven proved to be emotionally draining for Barnes because the Baroness embodied trauma. The Baroness, with her preference for dada, came to "encapsulate the pathology of the age, the trauma resulting from World War I." Mary Butts satirizes the relationship between the Baroness and Barnes in her 1933 short story "The Master's Last Dancing," in which she depicts an empress (the Baroness) dancing on the body of a character (presumably Barnes) until the character begins to bleed (Gammel 386). The intertextual relationship between the Baroness and Robin provides the war link necessary for an understanding of Robin's shell-shocked state. O'Connor only hints at the cause of Robin's dis-ease, but the comparison between the two figures confirms and solidifies the similarities while emphasizing the impact of war on female life.

Within *Nightwood* Robin receives a measure of sympathy from O'Connor; he suggests to Nora that Robin has been "purposely unspun" by some unspecified terror (107). O'Connor then proceeds to ask Nora for sympathy for Robin: "Don't you know your holding on is her only happiness and so her sole misery. . . . all the time what is Robin doing? Chucking Jack Straws, or sitting on the floor playing soldiers" (106). Exasperated with Nora's lack of empathy, O'Connor insists in hyperbolic fashion that Nora is Robin's "sole misery," which is certainly untrue. Robin is miserable and already damaged when she is first introduced in the novel, before she marries Felix and well before she even becomes acquainted with Nora. Nora may contribute to Robin's misery, but Robin's trauma stems from something unmentionable in the text. Even O'Connor is unable to define it. The problem with Robin's trauma is that it renders her incapacitated; she is reduced to playing with childish jackstraws and, tellingly, toy soldiers. As my comparison of Robin to the Baroness suggests, Robin's trauma harks back to World War I. In fact, Robin is compelled to reenact the source of her trauma when she plays with her toy soldiers.

As we see with Robin, the traumatized female characters in *Nightwood* behave in ways that highlight their emotional pain, even if they cannot articulate it. Jenny's violent attack on Robin in the carriage, in which she claws Robin's face until she draws blood, provides an instance of a physical, personal, and violent manifestation and response to emotional trauma. But it also mimics war on a microcosmic, domestic level. Jenny's unrestrained violence turns into an attack/battle with the intent of injuring; she wants to "win" Robin—and, surprisingly, she does in the next paragraph, through sheer brute force: "Slowly the blood began to run down Robin's cheeks, and as Jenny struck repeatedly Robin began to go forward as if brought to the movement by the very blows themselves, as if she had no will, sinking down in the small carriage, her knees on the floor, her head forward as her arm moved upward in a gesture of defense" (66). If one reads Jenny's attack as an allusion to war activity, with Robin as the (shell-shocked) somnambulist whose characterization is indebted to the (war-) victimized Baroness and who may be found "sitting on the floor playing soldiers" (106), then the close of "The Squatter" chapter does not seem so odd. Jenny has physically won Robin in battle; she assumes the behavior of a solider, mimicking the more literal war that they have all rather recently witnessed, and Nora the noncombatant loses her in the process. Robin's body is a battlefield, fought over and scarred throughout *Nightwood*.

In the brief, final chapter, "The Possessed," Robin succumbs to trauma and elicits a traumatic response that is both animalistic and semi-verbal. Before her breakdown, Robin retreats to the forest in an attempt to foster healing and reconnect with the living. In the process, however, Robin devolves into a bestial figure, almost entirely forsaking her negligible human identity: "Robin walked the open country . . . pulling at the flowers, speaking in a low voice to the animals. Those that came near, she grasped, straining their fur back until their eyes narrowed and their teeth bare, her own teeth showing as if her hand were upon her own neck" (137–38). This scene prepares the reader for Robin's breakdown and animalistic transformation.

The scene in the forest animalizes Robin's suffering body; she displays fear and aggression through bared teeth at the imagined feeling of being caught and held against her will, mirroring the animals' reaction to her. The fact that she feels as if her own hand were grasping her about the neck suggests that Robin is violently entrapped by her personal trauma, which produces the fear and aggression that motivates the battle in the final scene. Ultimately, Robin can speak her pain "in a low voice to the animals," but she is unsuccessful at communicating her trauma with the other characters or with the reader. Her suffering renders her almost incapacitated as a human; she is caught between two states: deathlike silence and animalistic behavior.

The scene in which Robin "goes down" with the dog depicts her "final attempt at communion with something living" (Scott 103). Robin crawls with the frenzied dog, barking with it, and "crying in shorter and shorter spaces, moving head to head [with the dog], until she gave up, lying out, her hands beside her, her face turned and weeping" (139). Construing Robin as the victim, *Nightwood* offers an anti-patriarchal depiction of a female response to trauma. As a victim presumably suffering from war trauma, Robin attempts a retaliatory battle with Nora's dog. Usually positioned as the victim of her own pain, Robin tries actively to fight back and engage in battle with the dog. The battle is her physical attempt at textual acknowledgment and represents a last performance of a traumatized female subject conflated with an animal in the text. As Robin suffers the effects of her breakdown, she communicates her embodied state through barking and weeping.[13] Even when she tries to tell her experiences in this female-authored avant-garde work, Robin can only perform actions that are extraverbal. Perhaps Barnes could not figure out a way for Robin to articulate her trauma coherently, yet Robin's silence and barking nevertheless form a powerful critique of phallogocentric politics in relation to women and war trauma. Her trauma is unspeakable. Women's responses to war trauma may traditionally be eclipsed by soldiers' accounts and male civilian war literature, but Barnes makes a statement in closing with Robin's weeping, thus foregrounding her suffering and the circumscribing effects of war trauma when suffered by a marginal subject.

The critiques in *Nightwood* are subtle and complex, which can produce misreadings, as Shari Benstock notes. Subjecting *Nightwood* to "patriarchal (critical) priorities," for example, "produced antilesbian readings . . . and made Robin Vote the perpetrator of evil in *Nightwood* rather than its victim" (Benstock 246). *Nightwood* critiques patriarchal practices and agendas such as war by exposing the mechanics of such operations as perverse and dangerous. Robin is not the perpetrator of evil; rather, she is the victim of a system that excludes her from recognizing the pain it has caused her. Robin is most certainly a victim because she suffers terribly as a result of her status as outsider; her war trauma is never fully recognized and acknowledged, because it cannot be articulated, and so she is beyond help.

Until the end female trauma continues to be figured as an embodied but animalized experience. Nora's dog reacts negatively to Robin when she begins her bestial transformation. The dog backs away from her, but Robin engages in battle, backing the dog into a corner and striking the dog in the side with her head. Lashing out, the dog bites at her, although he is terrified and whimpering and attempts to circumvent her and her trauma (139). The dog tries to avoid making contact with Robin, but she insists on battling it anyway. The male dog functions as an unwilling combatant and, as such, functions as a pseudo-soldier for Robin's hysterical mock battle. The battle is simply a reenactment of Robin's trauma and points to war as the source of Robin's breakdown. Robin continues to crawl after the dog until they fall into running together around the room. Eventually, the two collapse together upon the floor. The bizarre end of the novel offers no solution or remedy—except in the way of an engagement with war-related trauma and identity politics. The textual presence of Robin's breakdown and semi-vocalization of trauma interpellates women into war narrative without the use of proxy. But the fact that women's bodies in pain could not be directly accessed by the text until the very end—and even then in animalized, semi-vocal terms—constitutes the biggest critique of all. *Nightwood* addresses the marginalization of feminized bodies and the circumscription of female trauma, and the last scene featuring Robin's breakdown is the capstone of the novel's critique of phallogocentrism. The novel permits itself to render Robin's trauma partially visible.

Ultimately, *Nightwood* cannot be reduced to a strictly autobiographical account, a lesbian attack on patriarchy, or a didactic attack on fascism. *Nightwood* resists classifications in its endeavor to be a novel about war and homosexuality, about aberrant and acceptable performative behavior. It critiques the perversity of war and binary gender constructions through depictions of and stories about traumatic episodes. I argue that it is a novel that generates embodied responses to trauma and identity politics within the framework of war in order to critique war and exclusionary politics. It begins the work of inserting women into war narrative through allusions to female war-related trauma. Writing difference and the abject into her work, Barnes neither celebrates nor condemns but acknowledges the presence and trauma of marginal figures in the years between two world wars.

While Barnes records her emotional and psychological distress in her notes toward her memoir, her war novel takes an oblique approach. H.D., on the other hand, offers more direct treatments of war in her war novel and epic war poem. The main character of *Bid Me to Live* is a thinly veiled H.D., and the persona of *Trilogy* is H.D. the poet-prophet. H.D.'s poetics emerge in *Trilogy* in her representations of war and trauma, and thus it is compelling to examine both her role as a witness and her use of performative language in the epic poem. Embodying the role of poet-prophet in her response to World War II trauma and war narrative, H.D. creates a spiritual template for healing from war trauma and imagines feminist alternatives to patriarchal narratives. Unlike Barnes's pessimistic treatment of female war-related suffering in *Nightwood*, in her epic poem *Trilogy* H.D. offers a utopian alternative to war trauma, exclusionary politics, and patriarchal narratives.

CHAPTER 2

Validating Female War Experience through Literary Witnessing

The Poetics of the Poet-Prophet and the Politics of Trauma and Healing in H.D.'s *Trilogy*

An insistence on a female perspective defines H.D.'s war writing. Primarily interested in female subjects throughout her work, H.D. privileges the experiences and stories of women. *Trilogy* (1944–46), for instance, relies on first person literary witnessing, as does *Bid Me to Live* (1960). Like Djuna Barnes, H.D. writes corporeality and female identity into war narrative, performing female embodiment within a site of trauma. *Trilogy* authenticates female war experience through literary witnessing, insisting on an embodied presence in order to politicize women's bodies, women's stories, and women's suffering.[1] Recounting and reflecting upon personal trauma allows H.D. to validate suffering in personally political ways. Indeed, H.D. inscribes a place for her own personal trauma within the literary text *and* interweaves other women's stories to create an intertextual palimpsest, a layering and intermingling of stories and identities, that foregrounds feminist concerns, such as the exclusion of women from patriarchal narratives. H.D. carves out space in war narrative for the articulation of female suffering from trauma and conducts imaginative forays into the subsequent healing process by assuming and exploring the role of a poet-prophet, who strives toward wholeness and female empowerment through an expression of trauma and identification with a female community.

Wartime Trauma and *Bid Me to Live* as a Psychoanalytic Response to World War I

H.D. endured injury, loss, and severe mental distress during the World Wars, as her literary works (e.g., *Bid Me to Live* and *Trilogy*) attest. World War I proved devastating for her: in 1915 she bore a stillborn child as a result of war stress; in 1918, she discovered that her elder brother had been killed in action, with her father dying shortly afterward of a stroke; in 1919, H.D. and her estranged solider-husband, Richard Aldington, separated. On top of her amassing traumas, she also almost died at the end of the war of influenza. *Bid Me to Live* consists of a thinly veiled autobiographical account that details H.D.'s war experience. It provides a background to *Trilogy* in that it records her response to World War I, which informed her reaction to and reception of World War II. Indeed, *Bid Me to Live* foreshadows and predicts a future response to a future war: "She could not know that she was in the middle of a trilogy, she could not phrase it that way. She was in the middle of something. They all were. That war" (10). World War I did not play seamlessly into World War II, but the composition dates of *Bid Me to Live* allow H.D. to reflect upon World War I while in the midst of World War II. The First World War impacted H.D. to such an extent that World War II "acted like a second trauma to release a series of repressed memories. . . . In the re-enactment of a first trauma the repressed was supposedly released" (Buck 132). Claire Buck notes, "This psychoanalytic model of trauma and repression is H.D.'s model for both her output during the war years and after, and for *Trilogy* itself" (133). Conversely, H.D. biographer Barbara Guest and Donna Krolik Hollenberg, the editor of the letters between H.D. and Norman Holmes Pearson during World War II, assert that World War II was easier to bear than World War I for H.D. due to a variety of factors, including increased communication between soldiers and civilians. And yet letters written some time after the onset of World War II bespeak the emotional and physical strain H.D. suffered: she complains of "terrible face-aches" brought by "neuralgia or nerves from the blitz" (qtd. in Hollenberg 18). In 1946 H.D. suffered a physical and psychological breakdown due to war strain; Bryher describes her to Pearson as a "war casualty if there ever was one" (qtd. in Hollenberg 55). H.D. "was increasingly disturbed by the impending war" in the late 1930s and worked with Sigmund Freud and her partner Bryher to aid in the rescue efforts of Jewish people and to finance Jewish emigration (Barnstone 204). As a result, H.D. actively experienced the war from both a civilian viewpoint and the perspective of an active participant in the war relief effort, and her war experience permeates her literary output. All of her prose writing is autobiographical, and much of her poetry is self-referential (Guest xii).

H.D. sought psychoanalytic treatment for her war terrors from Freud, and her sessions with him led to the completion of *Bid Me to Live*. She describes her psychoanalytic treatment/study with Freud in *Tribute to Freud* (1956). She was an analysand from March 1933 to June–July 1933 (three or four months) and from October to December 1934 (five weeks), spending a hundred hours on the couch. Although seeking treatment for her own war trauma, H.D. considered herself a student of psychoanalysis as well. Ultimately, H.D. preferred to analyze dreams unrelated to war with Freud. According to H.D., she did, however, confide in Freud the details of her "severe shocks" during war, but he suggested alternate and what he considered to be more dangerous concerns for their review (*Tribute* 59). Even in the spring of 1920, after war had subsided, H.D. declares, "If I had been a little maladjusted or even mildly deranged, it would have been no small wonder" due to "unresolved terrors, perils, heart-aches, dangers, physical as well as spiritual or intellectual" (*Tribute* 60). The experience of World War I brought H.D. to Freud's door; she apparently wanted to prepare and fortify her psyche for the onslaught of another war. War was indeed on the horizon; H.D. encountered a swastika chalked outside of Freud's home, designating him as Jewish, upon a visit to him for psychoanalytic treatment. Following her sessions with Freud, H.D. wrote a draft of *Bid Me to Live* in 1939; the idea of *Bid Me to Live* was "provoked back into life by her analysis with Freud." H.D. completed the novel in 1949 (DuPlessis xx, 104). Additionally, the writing of the Freud memoir "slid easily between the last two parts of *Trilogy*, for *Trilogy* performs, in its way, a kind of analysis"

(Morris, *How to Live* 111). This observation underscores H.D.'s propensity to critique war and analyze her responses to it in critical ways. But *Bid Me to Live* and *Trilogy* provide very different treatments of trauma as a result of generic options and limitations. For H.D., the epic expansiveness of a poem like *Trilogy* becomes more conducive to exploring trauma *and* healing than the structure of an autobiographical, psychoanalytic novel allows.

War proves to be both a global and personal traumatic event that bars the possibility of quick convalescence, as H.D. witnesses in *Bid Me to Live.* In this novel H.D. foresees a hopeless future, devoid of opportunities for recovery and recuperation: "What was left of them was the war-generation, not the lost generation, but lost actually in fact, doomed by the stars in their courses, an actuality, holocaust to Mars, not blighted, not anaemic, but wounded, but dying, but dead" (8). Taking an almost naturalistic, fatalistic position, H.D. laments the injuries resulting from war that leaves an entire generation literally and metaphorically "dying" and "dead." Rather than rely upon the epithet "lost generation," H.D. renames the war-stricken population as "the war-generation," recognizing the undesired impact of war on soldiers' and civilians' lives. According to Rachel Blau DuPlessis, "*Bid Me to Live* and its study of the rupture of coequal genders because of the masculinist values derived from war exemplifies the consideration of militarism which is a unifying theme in H.D.'s work as a whole" (106–7). The study of war begets a study of gender relations, and H.D.'s war literature is engaged in exploring militarism precisely because of the gender politics underpinning the masculinist project of war. In her war writing, both in *Bid Me to Live* and, later, *Trilogy,* H.D. delves into both the "actuality" of war as she terms it and the "holocaust" aspect of war.

H.D. suffered terribly during war as a female civilian, and her depiction of female trauma is conspicuously personal in *Bid Me to Live.* In particular, she recounts air raids and her miscarriage during World War I: "Superficially entrenched they were routed out by the sound of air-craft; she stumbled down the iron stairs (that was the Hampstead flat) and bruised her knee. Just in time to see the tip-tilted object in a dim near sky that even then was sliding sideways and even then was about to drop. Such a long way to come. It drifted from their sight and the small collection of gaping individuals dispersed. Leviathan, a whale swan in city dusk, above suburban forests. My knee. It was a black gash, she might have broken her leg. . . . She had lost the child only a short time before" (*Bid* 11–12). The severely bruised knee and the miscarriage confession are both invoked by Julia Ashton, the H.D. figure, during the process of securing a safer place than her apartment during an air raid. Julia, like H.D., suffers both physical and emotional trauma; war marks its battles upon her body in the form of injuries (the knee and the damaged fetus) and in the loss of life (as represented by the miscarriage). The language in this passage bespeaks the correlation between civilian life and a soldier's life during wartime: at the mercy of attacks by the enemy, civilians are "superficially entrenched" until they are "routed out" by military machines and tactics. H.D.'s word choices denote women's involvement on the home front; as unwilling participants, they were sometimes exposed to dangers and experiences that could be compared to those of soldiers in superficial ways. H.D. is not arguing that female civilians suffered more than male soldiers, nor is she agitating for direct comparisons. What she is emphasizing is the potential for injury and suffering on the home front. For instance, while witnessing the air raid and descrying the descending bomb, Julia juxtaposes her impression of war activity with her own injuries, thereby underscoring the active suffering she is exposed to as a female civilian who is nevertheless "superficially entrenched" in the business of war as a business of injury.

Much of *Bid Me to Live* sets up *Trilogy*'s insistence on legitimizing and validating female narrative and female voice in connection with war and war trauma. But *Bid Me to Live* gives more space to the detailing of trauma, due to its novelistic, narrative form, than *Trilogy* allows. It foregrounds Julia's embodiment in connection with her psychosomatic responses to war: "Unconsciously, she was alert; she was waiting for the sound of the warning, of the air-raid warning. Her outer mind, frozen on the top, would go on quietly, this day and this day. But underneath, she was shot to bits—they all were—waiting for the end. The war will never be over" (71). Her body is attuned to war danger, the air-raid warning, and yet her "frozen" mind is unconscious of her body's alertness and subconscious mind's awareness. The language of this passage points to war activity, too; Julia's trauma is described as completely dismantling her defenses ("underneath, she was shot to bits" suggests being gunned down), rendering her—and other civilians—

helpless and primed for death ("they all were—waiting for the end") like an unprotected solider on the battlefield. The hopelessness Julia feels as a result of both her situation and the monotony of war is best expressed in her dejected realization that war will "never be over." The trauma Julia suffers is compounded by the continuation of the situation without reprieve and by the vulnerability of civilians during attacks on the home front.

The uncontained and undiscriminating nature of war is emphasized in *Bid Me to Live.* Female civilians do suffer during wartime because war cannot be contained as a male enterprise: "But as the war crept closer, as it absorbed everything, the thing that bound body and soul together seemed threatened" (68). H.D. calls attention to civilian and female embodiment in connection with war activity because the main problem with representations of war is the marginalization of civilians who are exposed to the trauma and injury that traditionally have been the province of male soldiers in war narrative. Women function within circumscribed roles in conventional war narratives, roles that reject any experience or knowledge of war. In rebuttal H.D. elucidates that women are victims of war (and thus do experience it) and even suggests that women may be the first and the most vulnerable victims during wartime: "men who might be ghosts to-morrow, the latest vintage (1917) grapes to be crushed. . . . There they all were. But she was already cast out, trodden under foot, she already had died. Already she was out of her body, she patronised them in her tolerance. She had escaped, was dead, they had that yet to do" (*Bid* 119). What is especially notable about H.D.'s diction is the focus on corporeality as a marker of trauma: Julia is excluded from acknowledged participation (through suffering) in war, even though she is the first here to suffer a broken body, as the metaphor of being trodden upon attests. And yet Julia assumes an attitude of patronizing tolerance because she knows trauma firsthand, which the soldiers of 1917 have yet to experience to the same degree.

The implication is that the soldiers will also be "crushed" and literally or metaphorically die, but Julia experiences it first and just as intensely. Finally, Julia turns away from an examination of her body because she already knows it to be injured; she is so traumatized, in fact, that she feels that she has "escaped"; she has nothing left to lose since she is, by her estimation, basically dead. Elaborating upon Julia's situation allows H.D. to recreate her own war trauma through literary witnessing since Julia functions as a stand-in for the author. As a result, H.D. writes a story that is meaningful to her in its psychoanalytic reworking of pain, but she proceeds to treat larger, philosophical issues, such as performative language.

In *Bid Me to Live* H.D. intimates the importance she ascribes to language in *Trilogy.* Words exert powers of transformation and carry a price: "The words themselves held inner words, she thought. If you look at a word long enough, this peculiar twist, its magic angle, would lead somewhere. . . . She was a trader in gold, the old gold, the myrrh of the dead spirit. She was bargaining with each word" (*Bid* 162). Myrrh (and by extension, language) becomes a symbol of renewal, points to the fertile female imagination, and transforms into a gift in "The Flowering of the Rod" of *Trilogy.* H.D. plays with language in ways that recursively allude to many women and their stories in order to perform a palimpsest that transforms patriarchal war narrative into a feminist narrative or treatment of war, trauma, and identity that foregrounds the importance of women and their stories. H.D. elaborates: "I would get something out of this war. But what I got out of this war isn't a Greek chorus-sequence. . . . No doubt, I will finish the sequence and tidy up some of my old lyrics. No doubt, another slim volume will attract the usual very small but discriminating public. But that isn't what I'm after. I want to explain how it is that the rose is neither red nor white, but pale gloire" (*Bid* 176). Avoiding the containment and exclusion of women that dictate binary relationships, H.D. bypasses an "either/or" situation by asserting that the rose—a poetic marker of female beauty, sexuality, and, ultimately, subjectivity—is neither one thing nor the other but something outside of conventional representations. H.D. clearly maintains that female identity does not rely upon gendered binary oppositions: "I could be Eurydice in character, you said, but woman-is-woman and I couldn't be both. The *gloire* is both" (*Bid* 176). Rather than produce another male poetic narrative about war in the form of "a Greek chorus-sequence," which would simply reproduce existing and circumscribing gendered binaries, H.D. vows to write a slim volume of war poetry that resonates with her older lyrics and yet forges new forays into depictions of female subjectivity (the "gloire"). *Trilogy* succeeds in meeting H.D.'s objectives for what the new feminist war poetry should look like.

The psychoanalytic roman à clef form of *Bid Me to Live* limits the scope of H.D.'s critique of war; traumatic episodes are presented and detailed, but the novel lacks the expansive scope of *Trilogy*. *Bid Me to Live* cannot look or move past trauma to explore a future narrative of healing and female empowerment, as *Trilogy* does, because of its insular focus and purpose. Although the actual composition of both works is somewhat contemporaneous, they were written for different reasons. *Bid Me to Live* evolved as an addendum and amplification of psychoanalytic treatment, while *Trilogy* assumes the position of the author's mature and artistic response to war and presents itself as a model for remedying the marginalization of women and their suffering in war narrative.

Performative Discourse: H.D.'s Poststructuralist Play with Language and Gender in*Trilogy*

Formerly titled the *War Trilogy*, *Trilogy* offers feminist responses to war trauma.[2] In order to portray women's war trauma, depictions that have been traditionally foreclosed, H.D. evokes performative language, a poetic poststructuralist play with language. According to trauma studies theorist Dominick LaCapra, "Writing trauma is often seen in terms of enacting it, which may at times be equated with acting (or playing) it out in performative discourse or artistic practice" (186–87). I equate H.D.'s poststructuralist play with language throughout *Trilogy* as a means to both write about trauma and to represent avenues toward healing. In *Trilogy* she enacts trauma and responds to it through what LaCapra terms "performative discourse"; she plays with representations by deconstructing images, infusing words and characters with new and multiple meanings and identities, and gesturing to older discourses (e.g., biblical narrative, Egyptian myths, and war narrative) in order to synthesize a new, feminist one to fit her artistic vision. Using performative discourse allows H.D. to present multiple aspects of trauma (e.g., devastation of landscape, personal suffering, and healing) that speak to her own female experience. Performative language allows her to come at the subject of trauma and gender from different angles; she can evoke more than one depiction, meaning, or perspective with a poststructuralist play of words and images that continue to suggest further possibilities of meaning and access because the chain of signifiers and limits of discourse are opened up, rather than closed, by H.D. Indeed, her employment of performative discourse and poetics (specifically, metaphors, metonymies, synecdoches, and H.D.'s own poetic creation, the palimpsest), treats the trauma H.D. experienced in literary terms and figures, thereby foregrounding several states of affairs at once through utterance and articulation: a topical treatment of women's war suffering by a woman and a generic template for a feminist rendering of war poetry.

The poetics H.D. uses constitutes performative discourse when it acts upon or delivers constructions of gendered identity; for instance, H.D. acknowledges in *Trilogy* that our understanding of Mary Magdalene is steeped in a traditional, masculine view of who she was and how she should behave as a woman; H.D. shows in "The Flowering of the Rod" that Mary is demonized because she thwarts patriarchal expectations. But H.D. reinvents and venerates Mary Magdalene through poetic devices when she conflates her with Mary of Bethlehem and various other female characters in the poem, thereby giving Mary a new identity that counters patriarchal expectations by opening up and sanctioning new ways to represent her. The two performative aspects of H.D.'s poetics, namely a poststructuralist play of language and a play with gendered acts and identity, foster an active awareness of the presence of female war trauma and women in war narrative. As such, the reader engages with issues pertaining to the marginalization of war trauma as experienced by women and the disenfranchisement of women from occupying legitimate space in war narrative and, broadly, patriarchal narrative. Writing war poetry allows H.D. to manipulate representations of gender and trauma; as LaCapra suggests in his definition of "performative discourse," H.D. reproduces the trauma she writes into her poetry in artistic ways, and I maintain that this writing out of trauma or enacting it in literary discourse validates and authenticates it in personally political ways, both for herself and for women collectively. In such fashion H.D.'s war writings offer a corrective to patriarchal war narrative by expressing female responses to war and opening up space for such responses.

Invoking trauma, especially if the trauma has been personally experienced, requires a distancing from the actual experience, whether through the reconfiguration of trauma in creative writing or through the healing process. Articulating trauma can be a therapeutic experience, but the nature of trauma is such that often traumatic responses from witnesses or survivors are foreclosed due to the extreme psychological and emotional wounding that accompanies it. Writing trauma "involves processes of acting out, working over, and to some extent working through in analyzing and 'giving voice' to the past—processes of coming to terms with traumatic 'experiences,' limit events, and their symptomatic effects that achieve articulation in different combinations and hybridized forms" (LaCapra 186). Through working out personal responses to trauma in her writing, H.D. pursues expression in various mediums (e.g., roman à clef and poetry) that allow her to articulate and work over trauma by witnessing and representing female suffering in different combinations: a psychoanalytic and reflective treatment of trauma in the form of the roman à clef and an epic treatment of trauma, marginalization, and healing in the form of poetry. H.D.'s experimental poetry allows her the breadth to introduce any subject she chooses, while her selection of the roman à clef limits her exploration to plot progression and the life of a single character. As a result, I will now focus exclusively on the epic three-part *Trilogy.*

Depictions of World War II Trauma in *Trilogy*

Of H.D.'s war writing, *Trilogy* assumes the position of a masterpiece due to its artistic maturity. The experience of two global wars informs *Trilogy,* and the work encompasses all of H.D.'s major themes and techniques: classicism, especially allusions to Greek and Egyptian goddesses; Imagist characteristics; feminist critique/rewriting of patriarchal narratives; celebration of feminine beauty; and psychoanalytic overtures. Composed of three long war poems, *Trilogy* presents three studies of war: a focus on trauma and destruction in "The Walls Do Not Fall"; an acknowledgment of the marginalization of women in war narrative and the need for female authors to witness/tell their stories in "Tribute to the Angels"; and a prescription for healing from trauma through woman-centered spirituality in "The Flowering of the Rod." Unlike the autobiographical and insular *Bid Me to Live,* which primarily concentrates on the life of a single woman, H.D. offers a sophisticated study of trauma in *Trilogy* that investigates the components of trauma and exclusion that pertain to women at large during wartime, while imagining remedies through poetic witnessing and a community of woman-centered spirituality and healing.

In her war writing H.D. emphasizes the dangers of life on the home front. She acknowledges the omnipresent threat of injury and death associated with World War I in *Bid Me to Live:* "She might say, London is the quietest place in the world, once it is quiet. Might have added, after an air-raid, everything, once it is quiet, is a graveyard; we walk among stones, paving-stones, but any stone might have been our tomb-stone, a slice of a wall falling, this ceiling over our heads" (15–16). When quietness ensues on the home front, it is an unsettling quietness that H.D. associates with the quietness of a graveyard, an apt comparison considering the fear of death and destruction left in the wake of bombardments. Air raids are a recurring image in H.D.'s World War II writing, and they are an appropriate image in terms of locating war within the domestic economy and female experience. The image of a World War II air raid closes "The Walls Do Not Fall" in *Trilogy:*

Still the walls do not fall,
I do not know why;

there is zrr-hiss,
lightning in a not-known,

unregistered dimension;
we are powerless,

dust and powder fill our lungs
our bodies blunder

through doors twisted on hinges,
and the lintels slant

cross-wise;
we walk continually

on thin air
that thickens to a blind fog
(58)

In spite of war ravages both the persona (which I read as H.D. in the guise of poetic witness) and the walls of buildings remain standing, much to the persona's surprise. The onomatopoeic *zrr-hiss* signifies the sound of a descending bomb, bringing the material reality of war onto the page while associating it with the female bodies of the persona and the author. Home has become "a not-known, / unregistered dimension" due to the effects of "lightning" bombardment, which leaves a noxious waste in its wake. Civilian bodies, probably female bodies (due to their proximity to domestic dwellings and the use of the collective *we* often signifies a community of women in *Trilogy* in the second and third poems) remain in peril ("dust and powder fill our lungs / our bodies blunder") and are rendered victims. The misshapen buildings ("doors twisted on hinges, / and the lintels slant / crosswise") speak to the possibility of bodily injury for the civilians in the next round of bombardment. The eerie image of a collective of (possibly female) bodies walking into a thickening "blind fog" suggests the dire straits and consequences in which unprotected civilian bodies are interpellated; these bodies are exposed to the unknown (the metaphoric "blind fog" that could also reference literal smoke from weapons) without substantial protection (walking "continually" on "thin air" suggests a lack of solid grounding or scaffolding, thus leaving one ungrounded, unstable, and vulnerable). Employing the language of witness with the use of a first-person persona and with references to a collective group of civilians, H.D. brings her war experience to bear upon the text metapoetically and thereby validates her own experience, while creating lines and images that resonate with authenticity.

Trilogy opens with the destruction of the domestic landscape, and this depiction sets the tone for the first of the three poems. H.D. invites the reader to participate in the construction of the scene by addressing the reader directly: "An incident here and there, / and rails gone (for guns) / from your (and my) old town square" (3). The first line almost dismisses the war battles as incidental, but the devastation wrought upon the persona's home carries metaphorical significance. Sarah H. S. Graham reads *Trilogy* as concerned with corporeality in this opening stanza; she interprets the human body as a frame and equates it with the walls of the poem title, "The Walls Do Not Fall," and the walls of buildings still standing (but missing roofs). In her interpretation Graham understands "rails gone" as a lack of protection for the vulnerable civilian body. Asserts Graham, "On a more symbolic level, too, the missing partitions that create 'inside' and 'out' can be applied to the body, whose physical shell—represented by the newly stripped 'town square'—is now in danger of being violated" (165). In this interpretation the building is a metaphor for the body on the home front. The images of physical structures are the poetic vehicle of the metaphor, and the tenor references human bodies. The allusions to corporeality underscore the actual physical dangers encountered by civilians like H.D. during wartime. *Trilogy* relies heavily on metaphor to convey physical, psychological, emotional, and spiritual trauma. In the earlier passage from "The Walls Do Not Fall" the destroyed landscape bespeaks the physical trauma wrought by war on both literal and metaphoric levels, but it also signals the potential for psychological, emotional, and spiritual suffering with the breakdown of boundaries between "inside" and "out," front lines and home front, and solider and civilian.

"Tribute to the Angels," the second poem of *Trilogy*, also strikes a comparison between the devastated landscape and corporeal and emotional trauma. H.D. uses the physical destruction of war to draw comparisons to and insist upon the bodily and emotional trauma experienced by civilians. Although the persona declares "from the visible / there is no escape" (86), she abruptly changes the subject with the help of an ellipsis (as if the subject were too painful to continue) after she identifies an old tree, barrel staves, bricks, and the remnants of a building that is remarkable for its "naked ugliness" (85). Set against the brief description of the ugly war-ravaged landscape are powerful images describing the persona's and her collective community's embodied trauma:

> a new sensation
>
> . . . .
>
> strikes paralyzing,
> strikes dumb,
>
> strikes the senses numb,
> sets the nerves quivering
> (85)

The damage inflicted upon buildings through war activity is obvious and uncontested. Juxtaposing confessions of a contested embodied experience of trauma on the same page with uncontested effects of war works to legitimize civilian, particularly women's, suffering as a result of H.D.'s persona of witness, during wartime. In this way, women's suffering is associated with war, defined as a destructive and injury-producing enterprise.

As a survivor, H.D.'s "body survived against the odds" (Graham 170), and *Trilogy* recounts the experience; H.D. is writing to survivors rather than eulogizing the dead. Her work is "ultimately a production for the survivors of cataclysm" (Detloff 258). As such, she chronicles and witnesses the survivor's fear of violation and annihilation. In a rare instance trauma is identified in corporeal language without an attachment to landscape:

> pressure on heart, lungs, the brain
> about to burst its brittle case
> (what the skull can endure!):
>
> . . . .
>
> the bone-frame was made for
> no such shock knit within terror,
> yet the skeleton stood up to it:
>
> the flesh? It was melted away,
> the heart burnt out, dead ember,
> tendons, muscles shattered, outer husk dismembered,
>
> yet the frame held:
> we passed the flame: we wonder
> what saved us? what for?
> (4)

As a result of the destruction around her, the poet questions her survivor status, implying that she has responsibilities as a survivor. In her response H.D. assumes the responsibilities of a female poet-prophet. This role requires much responsibility from H.D.'s perspective. In resurrection and healing practices female poets will lead the way: "Let us, however, recover the Sceptre, / the rod of power" (7). In effect power is a pivotal issue in feminist discourses and war narratives, and *Trilogy* assigns the power of vision and healing to women. The female poet-prophet thus emerges as a savior. According to Adalaide Morris, "Feminist literary criticism has so efficiently analyzed discourse about power because from the beginning it has participated in a politics that aims to change the ways we constitute and experience relations between the genders" ("Signaling" 130). In *Trilogy* power functions metapoetically; it references the power of the female author (H.D.) to create and witness, and it references the potential of the art form (poetry, *Trilogy*) to effect discursive and material change.

One discursive change *Trilogy* enacts is the rewriting of the war term *SS*. H.D. empties the term and reclaims it as a term of female spirituality and healing: "Ah (you say), this is Holy Wisdom, / *Santa Sophia*, the SS of the *Sanctus Spiritus*" (101). The Nazi Schutzstaffel (SS) was the elite guard of the Nazi state, made up of Adolf Hitler's most ruthless henchmen. The SS was synonymous with terror, its members charged with the management of concentration camps. The symbol of the SS was the double-S rune, or swastika, a symbol also synonymous with terror and destruction. Distancing herself from the murderous Nazi regime, H.D. symbolically empties the war term and rewrites it as a symbol of recovery and reclamation. As *Trilogy* editor Aliki Barnstone notes, "The SS is not a sanctifying of the Nazi SS or the Swastika—H.D. actively opposed Nazis—but a way of reclaiming her 'spiritual realism'" ("Reader's Notes" 190–91). According to H.D., "I distinctly link the LADY up with . . . the Byzantine Greek church Santa Sophia and the SS of the Sanctus Spiritus" (qtd. in Barnstone, "Reader's Notes" 190). H.D. links the Lady, a poet-prophet in "Tribute to the Angels," with a church and the Holy Spirit in order to enact a template that fosters healing from war trauma through female-centered narrative and spirituality. Through her direct commentary H.D. casts the *Sanctus Spiritus* as female or at least opens up space for female spirituality by drawing a connection to the Lady. In her association with feminist narrative and spiritual healing, the Lady, like H.D., embodies the poet-prophet role.

World War II presented H.D. with opportunities to explore the play and breakdown of language through poetic witnessing. For many trauma studies scholars the Holocaust "is the watershed event of the modern age because, uniquely terrible and unspeakable, it radically exceeds our capacity to grasp and understand it. And since this is so, the Holocaust is held to have precipitated, perhaps caused, an epistemological-ontological crisis of witnessing, a crisis manifested at the level of language itself." Although I do not wish to position H.D. within the Holocaust, I do want to frame her response to war within the framework of World War II. Language "succeeds in testifying to the traumatic horror only when the referential function of words begins to break down" (Leys 268). The horror of World War II is perhaps best expressed in the author's inability to describe it successfully. H.D. resorts to prompting her reader to consider her own experience rather than that of the persona/H.D.:

> what I mean is—
> but you have seen for yourself
> that burnt-out wood crumbling . . .
> you have seen for yourself.
> (84)

Throughout *Trilogy* H.D. tends to allude to war poetically rather than to describe it graphically. I suspect that this tendency is a result of what Leys characterizes as an "epistemological-ontological crisis of witnessing" that manifests itself in language. Rather than minutely describing or trying to taxonomize war, H.D. invokes it through allusions. Invocation, rather than description, also sidesteps the problem of desensitization. Instead of doling out graphic descriptions of war, H.D. asks her reader to experience the role of witness by using memory or imagination to (re)construct war in *Trilogy*.

Trilogy as a Reaction to Generic Patriarchal War Narrative

H.D.'s poetic use of the palimpsest exemplifies a feminist way of depicting experience and identity in her war poem that is in contrast to linear patriarchal war narrative. By definition a palimpsest is a trace; it evidences new work built upon old, as H.D. uses the term: "the same—different—the same attributes, / different yet the same as before" (*Trilogy* 105). Likewise, a poem stands in as "a trace, poem as evidence," especially if no other experiential representations exist (Forché 31). A plethora of female voices can be heard, expressing plurality and community, within the poetic, palimpsestic design of *Trilogy.* This framework brings together both new and old to form a collective female voice: "my mind (yours), / your way of thought (mine)" (51). *Trilogy* works to combat the linear discourse of patriarchy in war narrative through its superimposition of female identities and stories. H.D.'s epic poem is one of those "feminine texts . . . [that] strive in the direction of difference, struggle to undermine the dominant phallocentric logic, split open the closure of binary opposition and revel in the pleasures of open-minded textuality" (Cixous, qtd. in Moi 108). The palimpsest resists closure in its characteristic multiplicity and opens up space for an alternative treatment of war.

Powerful women populate H.D.'s palimpsest. Through the repetition of allusion the Egyptian goddess Isis becomes a significant figure in *Trilogy.* She attains goddess-hood through the god Rai's revealing of his name. Once Isis is able to name and claim Rai's identity within her own terms, she is elevated to the status of goddess. To name and therefore claim (the act of the witness) is a powerful act throughout *Trilogy.* The act of naming is powerful and empowering because it bestows identity:

> you would not have been, O Sword,
>
> without idea and the Word's mediation,
> you would have remained
>
> unmanifest in the dim dimension
> where thought dwells,
>
> and beyond thought and idea
> (18)

The one who names and narrates constructs or deconstructs identity within narrative. Without Logos calling objects into being, ideas and words remain "unmanifest in the dim dimension."

In the case of Isis a woman is elevated to the power of creator once she has the power to name the male god Rai and claim him within her frame of reference. The Christian God also possesses the power to name, equated with creation, as acknowledged by H.D.: "*in the beginning / was the word*" (17). This biblical reference suggests that perhaps there was a time when there was a perfect symmetry between signifier and signified, without all of the gaps that poststructuralist scholars identify and elucidate. H.D. implies, with her insertion of a biblical quotation in war poetry, that, even if wholeness had existed or ever been possible, war has successfully wrought fractures through its very nature as an enterprise begot by a breakdown in communication. And yet H.D. envisions a (re)turn to wholeness and healing in the third section of *Trilogy*, "The Flowering of the Rod," through the reclamation of female holy women and poets. God's words are invoked by H.D. to reify the power attributed to naming and to elevate principal female figures to deity status. Essentially, *Trilogy* is a feminist reinvention of Logos; the female poet-prophet possesses the awesome power to name, to claim, and to critique. A feminist invention of Logos is recreated through the act of naming by a woman; assigning women the ability and function of men, to name and claim, reinvents access and avenues to power, rather than simply inverting gendered positions. H.D. is not shifting the power from men to women in the Logos power play—such a move is impossible because men have enjoyed a long history of naming and claiming within historical, religious, and literary texts. Rather, H.D. opens up space for women as poet-prophets to participate in the male-dominated arena of poetry and literature, namely war literature.[3]

H.D. draws upon personal experience and the stories of other women to create a poetic palimpsest that challenges phallogocentric politics. Locating herself within the palimpsest framework as one of the poet-prophets, H.D. balances her personal viewpoint with a broader, female-oriented point of view: "I speak of myself individually / but I was surrounded by companions / in this mystery" (*Trilogy* 20). Specifically, H.D. calls upon pagan goddesses and biblical women and their stories for her overarching palimpsestic design. In an attempt to recover marginalized and disenfranchised mythic and historical women, she offers a corrective to patriarchal narratives through her valorization of the very same women. H.D. elucidates the ideas her palimpsest will work against:

> nor listen if they shout out,
> your beauty, Isis, Aset or Astarte,
>
> is a harlot; you are retrogressive,
> zealot, hankering after old flesh-pots;
>
> your heart, moreover,
> is a dead canker,
>
> they continue, and
> your rhythm is the devil's hymn,
>
> your stylus is dipped in corrosive sublimate,
> how can you scratch out
>
> indelible ink of the palimpsest
> of past misadventure?
> (5–6)

The persona instructs the pagan women she venerates through apostrophe to ignore the ways in which they have been criticized and subsequently marginalized: as promiscuous ("harlot"), as irrelevant ("retrogressive"), emotional ("your heart . . . / is a dead canker"), and evil ("your rhythm is the devil's hymn," "your stylus is dipped in corrosive sublimate"). These proposed faults are all gendered as feminine: conventionally, only women can be harlots and emotionally excessive, and female deities are understood as both retrogressive and evil from the male-centered biblical narrative. Prominent mythical and historical women have been written out of heroic roles and instead inscribed into "the palimpsest of past misadventure." As such, H.D. advocates a new palimpsest and new literature that favors rather than disenfranchises female subjects: "how can you scratch out / indelible ink of the palimpsest / of past misadventure?" In *Trilogy* H.D. delivers a reworking of generic patriarchal narrative that features a palimpsest of women, including the most obvious disenfranchised female subject in the modern world: the traumatized female civilian.

A solution to the disenfranchisement of women from war narrative requires that women respond to war artistically, and H.D. privileges the female poet-prophet as the necessary and crucial catalyst for positive change. The poet-prophet, like H.D., will create new feminist literary works that claim experience and envision avenues toward healing from trauma. The poet-prophet will prove that poets are practical and important, even though "the new heresy" of the 1940s views poets as "useless," "'non-utilitarian,'" and "'pathetic'" (*Trilogy* 14). War has no respect for high culture and humanity, attests the persona:

> though the burning of the books remains
> the most perverse gesture
>
> and the meanest
> of man's mean nature,
>
> yet give us, they still cry,
> give us books,
>
> folio, manuscript, old parchment
> will do for cartridge cases
> (16)

The example of burning books, the "most perverse gesture," correlates to H.D.'s opinion of war activity. Thus, the persona comments directly on the war enterprise when she condemns the burning of books as "perverse" and "the meanest / of man's mean nature." Without discrimination literature (and authors' lives) will be sacrificed for cartridge cases. Attempting to expose the baseness of war, the persona relies upon the image of burning books, a fitting image because *Trilogy* reveres the idea of the book as the appropriate forum for social change and for feminist discursive formations.

We can discern H.D.'s concern for literature as a platform for change in her focus on rewriting narrative and deconstructing binary constructions. The binary oppositions that underpin discursive formations are explored and exposed by H.D. In fact, the persona protests the violent circumscription of female trauma in war narrative. She sets up a binary relationship that seems to imply a gendered separation in the concepts of war trauma and war poetry:

> So, in our secretive, sly way,
> we are proud and chary
>
> of companionship with you others,
> our betters, who seem to imply
>
> that we will soon be swept aside,
> crumpled rags, no good for banner-stuff,
>
> no fit length for a bandage;
> but when the shingles hissed
>
> in the rain of incendiary,
> other values were revealed to us,
>
> other standards hallowed us;
> strange texture, a wing covered us,
>
> and though there was whirr and roar in the high air,
> there was a Voice louder,
>
> though its speech was lower
> than a whisper.
> (19)

What I interpret to be a female collective is opposed by "you others, / our betters," who dismiss the collective as garbage, "crumpled rags" that "will soon be swept aside." The female collective is thought to be unfit for the war effort ("no good for banner-stuff") and thus denied public acknowledgment of injury (the collective as "crumpled rags" offers "no fit length for a bandage"). The persona remarks, however, that, after experiencing the trauma of air raids ("the shingles hissed / in the rain of incendiary" and "there was whirr and roar in the high air") and after forming a collective ("in our secret, sly way, / we are proud and chary"), the possibility for creating and living an alternative narrative presents itself: "other values were revealed to us." The promise of new feminist narratives in validating female responses and experiences of war is strong: the female "Voice" drowns out the sound of the bombardment, even though the speech is modest.

The gender of the collective becomes apparent when the persona considers the dichotomy at the core of binary relationships. Addressing both a collective to which she belongs and a collective to which she does not belong, the persona explains that her collective is marked by "strangely encountered" and "strangely endured" peril. The displacement from war narrative during a time of war and the foreclosure of acknowledgment for trauma would beget strangely encountered and strangely endured dangers. Victims would be unable to receive appropriate treatment, and the victimization would be further compounded by the trauma of being rendered unimportant and invisible. The persona claims, however, that "we know each other / by secret symbols" (20), which can be taken as predictions of the new directions women's writing will take, perhaps in regard to war literature written by women about women. At present, according to the persona, her collective is "nameless" (21) and strangely silent ("though no word pass between us," we "do not speak at all" [20–21]). Buck explains that "in the process of investigating a history of women's cultural inscription H.D. typically formulates femininity as something unrepresentable and 'interdict' in the sense that it is something which never gets said" (132). Conventionally, representations of women or female embodiment in relation to war literature have been foreclosed.

In a catalogue of phrases the persona presents the following as poetic observations on female identity in connection with patriarchal narrative: "jottings on a margin, / indecipherable palimpsest scribbled over / with too many contradictory emotions" and "invasion of the over-soul into a cup / too brittle, a jar too circumscribed" (42). The violence of circumscription has been exact, leaving female authors nameless, speechless, confused, and marginal. The expansiveness of the over-soul, that site of Emersonian participation of the soul in the spiritual essence, or vital force, that transcends individual consciousness, is trespassed and contained in a brutal fashion ("invasion") for women in a "cup" that is "too brittle" to nurture it and in a "jar" that confines and prevents participation. "Invasion," as a war strategy, also indicates an occupation, a displacement and imprisonment. H.D.'s cup and jar metaphors for the unsuitable containment of women's agency alludes to the situation in which women writers and female civilians both found themselves. The war writing of women and the suffering endured by women during war have largely gone unacknowledged when compared to the accolades and simple acknowledgments bestowed upon their male counterparts.

Trilogy as a Poststructuralist Template for Feminist Spiritual Healing

Trilogy delves into the horrors of war, but H.D.'s poetic palimpsest of spiritual women (biblical women, pagan women, female poets-prophets) imagines a healing alternative to war trauma through validation of and identification with female-centered narratives. The Lady, who first appears in "Tribute to the Angels" and carries an open and unmarked book, functions as a redeemer: "she brings the Book of Life, obviously" (101). Others, especially artists and poets, please the Lady with their pursuit of art in the face of annihilation; the persona counts herself among the poet-prophets who are assigned the responsibility of inscribing the Book of Life:

> So she must have been pleased with us,
> who did not forgo our heritage
>
> at the grave-edge;
> she must have been pleased
>
> with the straggling company of the brush and quill
> who did not deny their birthright;
>
> she must have been pleased with us,
> for she looked so kindly at us
> (100)

The exact rhyme of *us* in this stanza emphasizes the artistic collective, and the two paired lines containing the first-person plural pronoun help to position the Lady as the figurehead of the (female) collective; the Lady's response to the artistic collective matters to the persona.[4] The Lady carries the "unwritten volume of the new" (*Trilogy* 103), and the possession of this book attests to her status as head of the poet-prophets: the Lady's "book is our book" (105). In particular, the Lady's narrative (her "book") counters the trauma engendered by war and war narrative from a female perspective. She represents "the counter-coin-side / of primitive terror" because she is "not-fear, she is not-war." In a sense she "is no symbolic figure"; she becomes real through her manifestation in the poet's book (104).

The Lady and the collective feel compelled to open up new possibilities for being. Problems stem from the trauma besetting the war generation: war has "Splintered the crystal of identity, / shattered the vessel of integrity" (*Trilogy* 30). While the subject or referent is literally omitted in the text, the word choices appropriately denote violent acts (*splintered, shattered*). H.D. laments "oneness lost, madness" (41). She argues for the dominance, or reign, of important (feminine) values that have been lost as a response to war trauma. Such values would champion a community of women and oneness and healing: "be cocoon, smothered in wool, / be Lamb, mothered again" (30). A new system is needed because "healing potions for the dead" and "new colours / for blind eyes" are superficial remedies that will not work (46).

This new system will be heralded by the poet-prophet/H.D., but under the heavy responsibility of naming and creating the poet-prophet quails:

> my patron said, "name it";
>
> I said, I can not name it,
> there is no name;
>
> he said,
> "invent it".
> (76)

But the poet must name because silence is the "metonymy of death" (Acheson 193). *Trilogy* keeps "death at bay by obsessively enunciating itself, spinning out words and adding more and more lyrics" (Acheson 191). H.D.'s vision consists of "an awareness of the 'spell'-ing and transformative power of poetry itself" (Zajdel 7), which can be witnessed in the line "mer, mere, mère, mater, Maia, Mary" (*Trilogy* 71). The word *mother* and the word *Mary* are positioned in such a way that they echo each other. The linguistic transformation of water to mother to Maia, the mother of pagan gods, to the biblical Mary(s) is an instance of metonymy effecting the palimpsestic design. The pagan Maia is given the positive attributes of the biblical Marys by metonymic association and is thereby transformed and reclaimed. Likewise, Isis is linked to Mary in the same way that the identities of Mary of Bethlehem and Mary Magdalene speak to each other. The palimpsestic design marries the stories and identities of pagan goddesses such as Isis to the biblical Marys in order to reclaim and venerate previously marginalized figures and stories. Various types of women are represented and reclaimed because H.D. apparently finds significance in recovery, in constructing an alternative history that provides women with more models and options for representation while embracing difference and unity. An alternate history provides choices for representation and behavior. Women's agency, behavior, and identity will become less constrained and contained with greater choices in terms of representation. In *Trilogy* H.D. refuses to denigrate any of the women she selects as characters in her epic poem; in fact, the denigrated women are elevated to the status of holy women, worthy of reverence. The conflation of different representations of women works to pool difference while insisting on a unified community. H.D. sanctions different performances by women to recover denigrated performances and marginalized characters from misogynistic bias and to offer a template of a community of unified but diverse women.

The signified mother (*mère, mater,* and *Mary*) explodes in a string of signifiers that run rampant in their allusions and performances of femininity in the performative "mer, mere, mère, mater, Maia, Mary." The effect of the metonymic string is a performance of ideas concerning who Mother Mary is; in other words, the idea of Mary or a mother is performative because the identity is grounded in repetitive performances of femininity and thus what it means to be, for instance, Mary—thereby sanctioning the performances as part of an identity. Metonymy prevents a single name and definition from solidifying because the signified mother becomes linked not only to *Mary* but to the other nouns evoked through the previous utterances. Indeed, H.D. invents a system of representations through metonymy that addresses issues of female representation, marginalization, and healing. Mary the "whore" is conflated with Mary, mother of Jesus, and both serve as synecdoches to the poet-prophet Lady. The string of signifiers gives a sense of openness and possibility through the endless malleability of the signifier. There is a sense of inclusion rather than exclusion, which fosters the wholeness that is integral for healing and for reclaiming, for example, marginal Mary Magdalene.

Certainly, the Lady is celebrated by H.D., but all of the female figures are valued equally and are sometimes depicted as extensions of the Lady or as part of a community in which the powerful Lady is the figurehead of the poet-prophets and the artistic collective. Significantly, the Lady resides in an even higher rank of angels than Gabriel: "I had been thinking of Gabriel . . . / how could I imagine / the Lady herself would come instead?" (*Trilogy* 92). The Lady once possessed widespread approbation: "you find / her everywhere (or did find), / in cathedral, museum, cloister / at the turn of the palace stair" (94). *Trilogy* reasserts her special status and importance. In effect attention is drawn away from the male baby in the person of Jesus to "the text, the book, with pages yet to be written upon" (Lucas 46), carried by the Lady in substitution for the biblical male baby and linear narrative.

"The Flowering of the Rod" continues the treatment of trauma and healing presented in "The Walls Do Not Fall" and "Tribute to the Angels." But this poem moves on to tackle the issue of resurrection as an antidote to trauma and paralysis, or stasis. The main point of section 7 of "The Flowering of the Rod" is that resurrection is "a sense of direction" rather than a destination (123). The resurrection is figured as necessary and constitutes a luxurious healing process associated with fragrance, myrrh, and balm. Balm is a significant ingredient because of its ability to soothe wounds; it underscores the theme of healing in "The Flowering of the Rod" as a whole. The addition of fragrance makes the healing process appealing, but myrrh is symbolic in "The Flowering of the Rod" and will be discussed later. In *Trilogy* the resurrection metaphorically stands for a turning in a new direction, following new philosophies, such as those presented by H.D. Luce Irigaray articulates a platform for the agenda that H.D. carries out: "What we need, we who are sexed according to our genre, is a God to share, a verb to share and become. Defined as the mother-substance, often obscure, even occult, of the verb of men, we need our subject, our noun, our verb, our predicates . . . . Woman needs a mirror to become a woman. Having a God and becoming his/her genre go together. God is the other of which we are totally in need" (qtd. in Lucas 45). Irigaray shows the play in male language that male signification denies and in which H.D. delights. H.D. accomplishes precisely what Irigaray deems necessary: she sets up her own genre, presents holy women who stand in as mother figures, makes use of obscure and occult references, and works within the language system / narratives of men to recreate what it means to know female experience and God as (M)other (Mother and Other). By linking God to the identity of Mother and Other, she ascribes female qualities to God, specifically that of caretaking. In this revision H.D. sanctions God as a Being who will nurture and protect women. She attempts to validate female spirituality by casting the highest spiritual Being as maternal.

(M)other as metonymy is best witnessed in the lines in *Trilogy* concerning the Marys. Mary of Magdala and Mary of Bethany are confused, their identities combined into a metonymic association:

> or was that Mary of Bethany?
> in any case—as to this other Mary
> (129)
>
> I am Mary, she said, of Magdala,
>
> . . . .
> I am Mary—O, there are Marys a-plenty.
> (135)

The use of metonymy stresses the performative element of gendered identity, portraying unity amid diversity through the performance of conflated identities that relate to and thus instruct and shape each other. Mary herself emphasizes the performative nature of gender in her reinstatement of who she is and her acknowledgment of other performances of being "Mary." In her second assertion, "I am Mary—O, there are Marys a-plenty," she withholds identification (i.e., which Mary is she?) and points toward the various possibilities opened for gendered performance by these very different women, linked only by name and sex. The marginalization of women in masculine narratives, as played out in the Christian narrative delivered in "The Flowering of the Rod," is resoundingly refuted. H.D. combats this marginalization by foregrounding the potency of Mary. H.D.'s Mary (namely, Mary Magdalene but also Mary of Bethlehem because they share a metonymic identity) withstands sexism, and she succeeds in offering herself as a gift of redemption.

The otherness of Mary(s), however, is foregrounded; she is described as an "unbalanced, neurotic woman, / who was naturally reviled for having left home / and not caring for house-work" (129). She is simultaneously revered by H.D. and reviled by history for behaving contrary to the patriarchal expectations of women. Her disregard for convention engenders the notion that she is a thief, stealing house money or the poor box money in section 12 of "Tribute to the Angels." Moreover, Mary

> knew how to detach herself,
> another unforgivable sin,
>
> and when stones were hurled,
> she simply wasn't there;
>
> she wasn't there and then she appeared,
> not a beautiful woman really—would you say?
>
> certainly not pretty;
> what struck the Arab was that she was unpredictable;
>
> this had never happened before—a woman—
> well yes—if anyone did, he knew the world—a lady

had not taken the hint, had not sidled gracefully
at a gesture of implied dismissal

and with no apparent offence really,
out of the door.
(131)

H.D. spends more time describing Mary than she dedicates to any other entity in *Trilogy*, as epitomized in the length of this excerpt. Hence, Mary should be viewed as a pivotal character. She is the first to witness Jesus' resurrection, which is why "The Flowering of the Rod," treating resurrection/healing (coming back to life literally and metaphorically), contains the most explicit poems concerning her. She is reclaimed by H.D. to star as a principal figure in the rewritten palimpsest of female power. The irony imbued in these poetic lines derives from the inequity in gender relations. Because Mary can survive independently of male imposed codes of behavior, she is othered. In the passage quoted here she is presented as unforgivable (having committed "another unforgivable sin"), unattractive ("certainly not pretty"), unpredictable, and unacceptable ("a lady had not taken the hint") when interpreted and measured against masculinist, traditional codes—namely, in regard to visibility and obedience, as this passage illustrates.

A patriarchal notion of sexuality also condemns Mary Magdalene to rejection and dismissal by the men of her time. In *Trilogy* what enables Mary to embody strength is her self-reflective knowledge that she is breaking gender constructs and refusing to participate in traditional masculine narrative:

she understood; this was his second rebuff
but deliberately, she shut the door;

she stood with her back against it;
planted there, she flung out her arms,

a further barrier,
and her scarf slipped to the floor;

. . . .
it was her hair—un-maidenly—

It was hardly decent of her to stand there,
unveiled, in the house of a stranger.
(134)

he handed her her scarf;

it was unseemly that a woman
appear disordered, dishevelled,

it was unseemly that a woman
appear at all.
(137)

Instead of disappearing from the narrative, Mary assumes a role tantamount to that of a principal figure. Instead of covering her body, she reveals herself. Mary's courage in becoming a spectacle through unveiling confronts old fears and begins the work of countering the old patriarchal narrative that excludes or denigrates her. Instead of disappearing from the text, Mary becomes the text; the focus in this passage is on her body, on its movement and appearance. The tone of the passage, however, concerns itself with representing Mary's body from the Arab's point of view. Judgment is passed on Mary's hair ("it was her hair—un-maidenly"), on her "unveiled" dress ("It was hardly decent of her to stand there"), and her overall "disordered" and "disheveled" appearance—culminating in the verdict that it is "unseemly that a woman / appear at all." The concern over Mary's appearance corresponds to concerns with chastity. Understood to be a harlot, Mary's appearance underscores her putative immorality, her "disordered" morals. H.D. frames Mary's body within this traditional framework of contained female sexuality in order to demonstrate how Mary Magdalene has traditionally been construed in texts.

Because H.D. casts Mary as the embodiment of female spiritual healing, Mary Magdalene's physical body becomes a trope of a consciousness for resistance and transformation in "The Flowering of the Rod." The presentation of Mary's body works through metaphor. Her act of closing the door represents defiance on many levels, not simply a physical separation of her person from another. The crucifixion stance she assumes, back against the door with arms flung out, begs an allusion to Jesus. She represents a barrier to masculine-centered theology. Mary's unveiling emphasizes her body as spectacle/text, but the tenor of the body metaphor points to Mary as a receptacle for a different kind of spirituality from that which excludes her. The palimpsestic design recovers Mary Magdalene from venery and reinstates her as a virtuous women in her own right. *Trilogy* ends with Mary cradling myrrh, thereby emphasizing the healing that accompanies the inclusion and veneration of women in religious narrative. Mary equates herself and Mary the mother of Jesus in the metonymic "Mary-myrrh" (135). Biblically, myrrh is featured as a principal ingredient in holy anointing oil, and it is included in the gifts brought by the wise men for the baby Jesus. Traditionally, then, myrrh has functioned as part of a blessing and as a gift. Dennis Brown concludes that myrrh is the "main symbolisation" in *Trilogy* (356), arguing that it is the most important image (despite the fact that he is unclear about what the myrrh itself represents). As metaphoric myrrh, I contend that Mary offers herself as a healing gift, a gift indebted to biblical narrative and the agenda of *Trilogy*.

H.D. takes up a feminist agenda in connection with war narrative in *Trilogy:* in it she extols the feminine by representing various and diverse women as well as advocating witnessing and employing feminist narrative strategies. These strategies include advocating for the acknowledgment of multiple identities; focus on female characters and experiences; and presentation of female characters as active heroines (the poet-prophets and the Marys as figureheads for spiritual healing and visionary narrative gifts). *Trilogy* is certainly a feminist work that enacts what it envisions. DuPlessis describes H.D. as "an anti-patriarchal symbolist" who yearns "for centre and presence" (89). Indeed, Mary is the anti-patriarchal symbol that H.D. invokes in her quest to rewrite masculinist history. Female characters are the heroines in her palimpsestic framework, a framework that insists on the presence of women through allusions to corporeality and features them in the very center of narratives, a position previously occupied by men. Michael Hardin argues that the body of "Mary Magdala is the palimpsest" on which the Christ narrative is most dramatically altered (159). The focus of the revised biblical narrative to a large extent pivots on Mary in *Trilogy;* she even becomes myrrh, transforming herself into a gift in the same way Jesus does. Thus, history is rewritten not only to accommodate women but to feature them as active participants who are worthy of recognition in narratives featuring war and trauma.

In her introduction to the collection *Against Forgetting: Twentieth-Century Poetry of Witness* Carolyn Forché asserts that we need to read with an erasure of boundaries between the personal and political ("the social") in order to read the literatures of trauma effectively (31). In this vein poetry can be read as a vehicle for protest and resistance. Suggests Forché, "But perhaps we should not consider our social lives as merely the products of our choice: the social is a place of resistance and struggle, where books are published, poems read, and protest disseminated" (31). Poetry is political; it can authenticate and potentially give public value to female perspectives. Representation becomes especially crucial in regard to trauma because victims are rendered powerless and the powerless are rendered invisible. Thus, accounts of trauma by women are necessary for empowerment—personally and politically. In *Trilogy* H.D. offers literary accounts of witnessing trauma, and she epitomizes Forché's observation that "the social is a place of resistance and struggle." H.D. weaves lived experience within a work concerned with narratives of trauma and marginalization in order to explore avenues toward healing and exposure.

Reading accounts of others' experiences of trauma allows for insight into the process of suffering and healing while providing an affirmation of survival. Indeed, "language, if nothing else, can resist both sudden trauma and gradual decay. The word affirms that, amid falling buildings, a poem exerts a sturdy constructive force" (Boehnen 181). H.D. witnesses the trauma of war, and it is precisely because of her feminist treatment of trauma that *Trilogy* is exemplary. In her epic poem H.D. considers the traumatic experience of war and appraises the role of the female poet in conjunction with trauma and its alleviation. Witnessing allows terrors to surface, and H.D. channels those terrors into a therapeutic catharsis while suggesting further sites or processes of healing. On February 8, 1944, H.D. wrote, "I have never worked so hard as in the past few years—a terrific creative urge that, I suppose, is a sort of 'escapism' but a cerebral drug, too that has kept me sane and alive—the writing is crazy, if you will—but has acted as a sort of safety valve" (qtd. in Hollenberg 19). In short writing out her trauma allows H.D. to present the traumatic experience of war in personally meaningful ways and allows her to investigate avenues toward healing from a feminist perspective. *Trilogy* validates the experience of a female civilian while revisioning the world in feminist terms. It enacts a female-centered poetic template that legitimizes female war trauma and marginalization and creates space in war narrative for empowerment and spiritual healing through identification with a female community.

In *Trilogy* H.D. foregrounds a personal, female response to war, trauma, and marginalization when she assumes the role of poet-prophet and metapoetically references her own experience. Like H.D., Gertrude Stein brings her own experience of war to bear upon her literary work, but Stein's experience of war in occupied France keeps her strangely removed from the trauma of brutal attacks that H.D. endured in London during the Blitz. Throughout her war writings Stein focuses on the quotidian aspects of life as a strategy for surviving war, yet indirectly she responds to the disruption and terror of World War II. And yet the voice of the embodied female survivor in her 1952 novel *Mrs. Reynolds* is explicitly a female voice in wartime.

CHAPTER 3

A War Heroine in the Domestic Economy

The Embodied Female Survivor in Gertrude Stein's *Mrs. Reynolds*

Unlike Djuna Barnes, Gertrude Stein comments explicitly on her war experiences at great length. She also discusses her personal experience with war much more directly than H.D. through her autobiographical accounts of life during World War I, although Stein also fictionalizes her experience of World War II in *Mrs. Reynolds* (1952) in a manner that is somewhat similar to H.D.'s *Bid Me to Live*. Both novels rely heavily on each author's experiential knowledge of war, and both code personal experience and observations with thinly veiled characters: just as Julia Ashton is a stand-in for H.D., Mrs. Reynolds is the fictional counterpart for Stein. In regard to the other authors featured in this study, Stein's treatment of war is the most extensive (due to her copious writing on war) and the one that is the most grounded in the mundane details of managing life in the domestic economy.

For the most part Stein was strangely removed from war violence in spite of the fact that she lived in occupied France as a lesbian Jew. As a result, Stein's experience of war differed from H.D.'s in that Stein's major concerns during war revolved around domestic needs, like foraging for food, rather than securing shelter from aerial bombardments, though Stein was familiar with bomb shelters. For Stein war translates into problems for the managers of the home: food scarcity, curfew, and limited luxuries. The quotidian concerns of civilian life in wartime are given primary focus; Stein attempts to distance her female characters and narrative voice from trauma by concentrating on the mundane. Yet there are moments in the text in which a sense of a traumatized civilian emerges, and the dangers and threats of bodily harm associated with war in general and living with the enemy during occupation in particular are articulated and repeated in ruptures of the narrative voice in Stein's war texts. The emphasis on the daily details of civilian life during war bespeaks the recurring themes in her war writing: women as sufferers and survivors. Along with Barnes and H.D., Stein insists on women's presence and corporeal vulnerability during wartime through gestures to and acknowledgments of women's bodies. Stein's response to generic patriarchal war narrative manifests in Mrs. Reynolds, the embodiment of a war survivor and the fictional proxy for Stein herself, as corroborated by Stein's other war texts.

Lifting Belly as a Literary Precursor to *Mrs. Reynolds*

Stein's experience of World War I is embedded in the long poem *Lifting Belly* (composed between 1915 and 1917 and published in 1953). I have selected *Lifting Belly* instead of "Marry Nettie: Alright Make It a Series and Call It Marry Nettie" (1917) for discussion because the sixty-two-page *Lifting Belly* constitutes a more developed response to the intrusion of war on domestic life, and so it contextualizes Stein's war writings more effectively than the somewhat similar (in terms of domestic concerns, time period, and location) five-page prose poem, which is written in the style of *Tender Buttons* (1914). Neither *Lifting Belly* nor "Marry Nettie" is about war exclusively, but both reference war obliquely in a domestic context. The design of *Lifting Belly,* however, foreshadows the agenda Stein would later execute in *Mrs. Reynolds:* a rewriting of patriarchal narratives—namely, generic war narratives and literary forms—to include and foreground women and female literary work about war experience. The major difference between *Lifting Belly* and *Mrs. Reynolds* is the focus. *Mrs. Reynolds* offers a female perspective of war and delves into the gendered nature of war experience by chronicling the life of a female civilian. *Lifting Belly,* however, is not about war so much as it is about lesbian sexuality and eroticism, although it incorporates war references, and war becomes the backdrop of the poem. This poem is an important precursor to *Mrs. Reynolds* because it shows Stein already thinking about war within the realm of domestic experience.

Lifting Belly presents an experiment on the traditional love lyric. Stein reconfigures the conventional lyric (in which men gaze upon their beloved, number her qualities, and lament that she is unattainable or unfaithful) and completely subverts it to celebrate lesbianism: the gaze is unfixed, and the celebration takes place in a sexual sphere. Although *Lifting Belly* has the trappings of a heterosexual love lyric, Stein deconstructs the generic conventions in order to foreground lesbian sexuality and the reality of war impinging on an otherwise idyllic love and life. There were no models for this sort of poem, and Stein's work is innovative and significant because it carves out generic space for her and Toklas, with an insistence on female bodies occupying erotic and sociopolitical spaces.

Begun in 1915 in Palma de Mallorca, Spain, the first untitled section and the section titled "PART II" of *Lifting Belly* unfold in Mallorca. The sections entitled "II" and "III" are set in Paris, France, and the setting of these sections correspond to the move Stein and Toklas made in June 1916. By the next March Stein and Toklas were actively participating in the war effort as supply transporters and hospital workers for the American Fund for the French Wounded (AFFW). To some extent *Lifting Belly* invites an autobiographical reading, but to read it strictly autobiographically would produce a reductive reading. Besides, the reader who attempts to read *Lifting Belly* only as autobiography will be frustrated. According to Margaret Dickie, "Revealing the details of the public war was as taboo [for Stein] as revealing the details of her private erotic life" (48). When Stein offers a personal detail from her erotic life with Toklas or when she offers a historic detail about the war, she immediately undercuts the transparency and perhaps even the facticity of the work by juxtaposing nonsensical material with the readable or translatable coded material.

Early in the poem, for instance, Stein writes, "When we read about a boat we / know that it has been sunk" (1–2).[1] Because *Lifting Belly* is set against the backdrop of war, the reader already familiar with this aspect of the work will discern that this line is the first reference to war. David M. Owens links this reference to "the German policy of unrestricted submarine warfare and newspaper accounts of attacks on such vessels as the *Lusitania* in 1915" (610). Stein follows this war allusion, however, with the following lines: "Not by the waves but by / the sails. Any one knows that rowing is dangerous" (2). These lines are confusing, even though they seem to provide further elaboration. Of course, sailboats are not warships, and sailboats do not sink as a result of damaged sails. So this information could be a coded way of talking about war, or it could have nothing to do with war whatsoever; the lines are purposely ambiguous. On the other hand, rowing a boat may very well be a dangerous activity during wartime because civilians are exposed and vulnerable on the water, but Stein does not offer an explanation about what she precisely means. But the war spin of this interpretation appears valid because of the proximity of the line to the more overt war reference—not because Stein decodes or reductively tells us how to read.[2] The persona of *Lifting Belly* is not interested in discussing war directly, and this indirect treatment correlates to Dickie's notion of World War I as a taboo subject for female authors.

Stein includes women in the war effort by interweaving her lesbian love lyric with war references;[3] the female body is invoked and transposed into war narrative through the conflation of domestic images and war references. I am not suggesting that Stein polices a kind of absolute divide that positions women firmly in the domestic realm and thus renders them unable to cross over to more public, masculine spaces. Indeed, Stein references the Ford automobile, nicknamed Aunt Pauline, that she drove for her AFFW work, and the Englishwoman is traveling *with* the Englishman in the following lines, which illustrate the transliteration of female bodies into war text:

> The Englishmen are coming. Not
> here. No an Englishwoman. An Englishman and an
> Englishwoman.
> What did you say lifting belly.
> (3)

Owens suggests these lines allude to "news of the British Invasion at Gallipoli, Turkey[,] in the spring and summer of 1915" or, at the very least, a reaction to news of "events on the stalemated Western Front" (610–11). If the Englishmen represent soldiers, then the "Englishwoman" is drawn into the war situation by association. At first Stein denies the woman's presence in war activity, and then she affirms her presence by stipulating that both an Englishman and an Englishwoman will arrive somewhere other than "here" together. Stein links the Englishwoman with war activity by association if we read the Englishmen in the passage as soldiers in transit, on their way to engage in war activity. The linking of *lifting belly* to the impending arrival of English citizens/troops suggests the intrusion of war into the "here," or home, of "lifting belly."

The veiled war references play into Stein's design to juxtapose war with domestic life and lesbian sexuality. Immediately following the announcement of the "troops," Stein invokes *lifting belly,* a noun, sometimes a verb, that refers to various aspects of lesbian sexuality and eroticism and is usually located within the domestic sphere. Elsewhere in the poem, however, the phrase is tied to war activity and strength:

> A great many people are in the war.
> I will go there and back again.
> What did you say about Lifting belly.
> I said lifting belly is so strong.
> (6)

"Lifting Belly" is here implicated in war discussion; the speaker of the poem notes that numerous people are helping out with the war relief effort, and she plans to travel to offer her aid. Following this allusion to war relief work, Stein juxtaposes concern about how *lifting belly* is discussed: "What did you say about Lifting Belly." The speaker ensures that she understands the terms in which *lifting belly* is invoked. In this passage *lifting belly* signals strength ("I said lifting belly is so strong"); it is used as a noun, attributed with a physical attribute. Here the invocation of *lifting belly* connects war and the female body, with an emphasis on the physicality of female bodies. Thus, in this section *lifting belly* emerges as the embodiment of (female) strength.

Throughout the poem as a whole *lifting belly* is defined numerous times and in such varied contexts that it ceases to refer to one specific thing, person, activity, or state of being. The indeterminacy of what *lifting belly* signifies begins the work of deconstructing expectations concerning logocentric conventions that background lesbian sexuality and women's responses to war in literature. This indeterminacy plays into Stein's deconstruction of patriarchal terms, rhetoric, and narratives—namely, in relation to the love lyric and war narrative. In many instances *lifting belly* connotes physicality or stands in as a physical symbol. The name itself suggests a body part engaged in action. When *lifting belly* is mentioned in reference to women's bodies or physicality, it references a textual body, usually that of the speaker of the poem or her companion. It can be representative of anything pertaining to lesbian identity, but Stein emphasizes its textual nature: "Lifting belly is alright. / Is it a name. / Yes it's a name" (5). This affirmation of the textuality of *lifting belly* follows a not-so-veiled section on sexual activity. In these lines the term functions as part of a textual body (a noun or thing that is "alright" and that has previously been engaged in sexual relations), but Stein emphasizes that it is textual in nature, as her insistence that it is a name (a signifier), instead of a concrete object (a signified), suggests. Thus, *lifting belly* is a name that can signify differently at different times.

Rather than objectifying the female body, Stein invokes it through the slippery noun/verb *lifting belly.* Nicola Rehling observes, "Stein attempts to tease out the rigidity of the noun and, in 'caressing' it, she engages the body in writing" (79). There is a direct correlation between Stein's language play and her deconstruction of traditional or conventional roles for the female body. Invoking corporeal presence is important in *Lifting Belly* because the female body takes on new dimensions in the text: the textual body insists on its presence in a lesbian relationship and in war simultaneously. Furthermore, linking the female body with war experience or knowledge is an important first step in claiming space in which to acknowledge suffering female bodies. Stein can neatly switch from a scene of lovemaking to war and back again through the shared landscape of the female textual body. The female body is the site on which Stein pins sexual and political tensions.

Lifting Belly anticipates the concerns of everyday life, positioned within the domestic economy during wartime, that are best depicted in *Mrs. Reyn-*

olds. One such practical concern is the deprivation caused by food rationing. The poem's speaker wonders, "And is there any likelihood of butter" (61). War makes its presence known not only through deprivations but in interruptions as well. Interspersed with discussions of lifting belly within the domestic life are snatches of and references to "The Star Spangled Banner." In this particular passage the love lyric is interrupted by an allusion to war:

> Lifting belly is not so kind.
> Little places to sting.
> We used to play the star spangled banner.
> Lifting belly is so near.
> Lifting belly is so dear.
> Lifting belly all around.
> Lifting belly makes a sound.
> (13)

The association of "The Star Spangled Banner" with the persona signifies the American identity of the persona and her companion, thus affirming national identities at a time when national affiliation matters politically. At the same time, the persona attempts to shut out thoughts about war music and concentrate on lifting belly instead. The persona insists on focusing on her partner in spite of obvious distractions: "Red white / and blue all out but you" (19). The war, however, continues to interfere with love and the writing of lyric poetry about love by making its presence known through interruptions. Another example follows: "Lifting belly is so kind. / What is a veteran" (22). The abrupt insertion of war references into the love lyric replicates the actual interruptions of civilian life due to war concerns and impositions.

The second half of *Lifting Belly*, set in Paris, mirrors the increased presence of war. Anticipating her war work, the female persona states in the Mallorca section, "A great many people are in the war. / I will go there and back again" (6). Stein and Toklas, after the arrival of Aunt Pauline, could travel "there and back again" as part of the war relief effort. With the help of the Ford automobile, they aided in opening a supply depot on March 18, 1917 (Bridgman 154). Stein writes in *Lifting Belly*, "It is necessary to have a

Ford" (22). The automobile is important to Stein because she and Toklas used it to insert themselves into the war effort. In a sense they were active participants in World War I because they were engaged in war business in the form of relief work. With her participation in the war effort, Stein "began to see herself not only as a nurturing and maternal figure, an image latent perhaps in her early writing and now available as an imaginative strategy as well, but also as an active participant in the essentially male war effort" (Dickie 41). In *Lifting Belly* and especially in *Mrs. Reynolds* Stein reconfigures the war effort to be one of male *and* female participation.

Yet what constitutes male and female essentialist characteristics is deconstructed in both war works by Stein. The following declaration is found in *Lifting Belly:* "Some are wives not heroes" (21). It follows, then, that some must be heroes and not wives, and perhaps some can be both. Given the context of the poem, *heroes* resonates with a specific kind of hero: a war hero. Conventionally, a war hero denotes a man—but war heroes, Stein seems to imply, can also be wives and thus women. Later on, Stein actually questions essentialist identities in the poem directly: "What is a man. / What is a woman. / What is a bird" (35). She refuses to address her questions posed like declarative statements, perhaps because they are unanswerable; in Stein's work there is not one way to be a "man" or a "woman." In glossing over the questions, Stein trivializes them. She refuses to give them any serious consideration, and she further trivializes the essentialist topics by introducing the bird's identity as a questionable element. The addition of the bird to the list undercuts any seriousness attached to the previous subjects. Moreover, the previous questions become reconfigured by association with the bird question; birds do not mark gender boundaries, and so, ultimately, in this passage Stein prompts the reader to begin to deconstruct gender identity when she pushes the reader to reconsider the configuration of gendered identity. Probing into the nuances of *heroes* and *man* and *woman* allows Stein to unsettle definitions. In deconstructing gender in connection with war, Stein opens space in her literary works for affirmation and validation of women's presence in wartime and, by extension, women's work in wartime. Women can be "heroes" too in Stein's revised lexicon.

While Stein allows that women can be heroes, she also acknowledges that fear and anxiety are part of life in wartime for her female characters. Fear and anxiety are palpable in *Lifting Belly*, but these emotional states are not as intense as they are in *Mrs. Reynolds*. Nevertheless, the persona worries because lifting belly can be damaged or victimized:

> Lifting belly the dear.
> Protection.
> Protection
> Protection
> Speculation
> Protection
> Protection.
> (61)

The repetition and foregrounding of *Protection* (the word is given its own line five times) underscores the almost overriding worry the persona harbors for the welfare of lifting belly and, by extension, her companion. (Indeed, *lifting belly* can often be read as a synecdoche for the companion, especially when lifting belly is addressed as a person.) The war continues to unnerve the persona's companion, though there is an attempt at distancing lifting belly from the bloodshed of battle. On one occasion lifting belly is depicted as anxious, but the persona protests that the anxiety is not produced by the Battle of Verdun: "Lifting belly is anxious. / Not about Verdun. / Oh dear no" (8). The French eventually won the battle against the Germans, but the conflict, lasting from February 21 to December 18, 1916, resulted in nearly one million casualties (Owens 611). The Battle of Verdun may, in fact, cause lifting belly anxiety if the persona were honest with the reader and herself. The adamant denial ("Not about Verdun. / Oh dear no") is too strong of a protest and suggests that the persona may simply be unable to admit the very real impact of the battle upon lifting belly. Allusions to uncertainty and fear remind the reader that these emotional reactions are responses to a very real historical situation.

The anxiety generated in this poem is on a smaller scale when compared to the anxiety and fear depicted in various sections of *Mrs. Reynolds*. The reason for this discrepancy may be traced to Stein's increased exposure to war activity during World War II. Stein and Toklas did not see much of World War I firsthand, according to Richard Bridgman: "During the actual war, their assignments were all in the southern regions of France, well away from the fighting" (154). Although Bridgman reads *Mrs. Reynolds* as being set in unoccupied France (319), Stein and Toklas did experience and live through occupation, and *Mrs. Reynolds* captures the trauma of war and the mind-set of war in a more direct and experimental manner than *Lifting Belly*, simply because the threat of war during the *Lifting Belly* years was not as present and dangerous for Stein as it was during the years of writing *Mrs. Reynolds* or *Wars I Have Seen* (1945).

World War I and World War II constituted two different experiences of war for Stein, the long poem *Lifting Belly* being a literary precursor to the novel *Mrs. Reynolds*. The poem acknowledges the interference of war on domestic life, articulates intermittent fear and anxiety, inserts female characters with corporeal concerns into war narrative, and deconstructs gendered expectations for war narrative through language, primarily through the revision of a war lexicon (e.g., *hero* and *lifting belly* in *Lifting Belly* and *soldier* and *veteran* in *Mrs. Reynolds*) and through language play that destabilizes definitions.

Mrs. Reynolds and the Rewriting of Patriarchal War Narrative

The patriarchal war narrative of World War II is addressed and reconfigured in Stein's *Mrs. Reynolds*, published posthumously in 1952 but probably written during the years 1940 to 1943.[4] Stein's depictions of Mrs. Reynolds and her mind-set reinforce the revisioning of the war as an activity or battle that was actively engaged in on the home front by women. The desire to claim the war as part of female experience challenges a patriarchal vision of history and literature. In her war writings Stein writes women into historical accounts of war as active players, but she also experimentally re-creates the mental states of ordinary, noncombatant characters. While trauma is marginally invoked in *Mrs. Reynolds*, the novel is more about war narrative and representations of war and responses to it by a female civilian. In *Mrs. Reynolds* Stein contests notions of a dichotomy between war and domesticity, all the while interweaving her feminist narrative of World War II with complex inquiries into the gendered constructions of war, identity, and language.[5]

Developing a plot summary for *Mrs. Reynolds* is an almost impossible task because the novel does not have a plot. Rather than developing a story line per se, Stein focuses on quotidian details of Mrs. Reynolds's life and responses to war. In an attempt to inform herself about war, Mrs. Reynolds seeks news, sometimes desperately and sometimes in a hesitant manner, because the effects of war are felt on the home front. But the novel mostly captures the mind-set of Mrs. Reynolds as she lives through war. Mrs. Reynolds is, by turns, anxious and exhausted through the duration of World War II. The monotony of waiting for news and the cessation of warfare prove exhausting to both Mrs. Reynolds and the reader: "They wanted to know what the news was, but after all, it would do just as well to know the news tomorrow as today. In every way the news was the news of yesterday, and yesterday was another day and so was tomorrow" (88). It is this monotony to which *Mrs. Reynolds* pays special attention. Rather than positioning Mrs. Reynolds as a witness to actual battles, Stein renders her main female character as a witness to the mind-set of life on the home front. Her responses to war include conjectures about the cessation of warfare (which turn into extremely repetitive thoughts about the passing and marking of time), slight protestations about the hardships of war, and professions about the accuracy of prophecy. Throughout the novel we encounter hints that Mrs. Reynolds may be traumatized, mainly in her recurring thoughts on death, injury, and relocation and in her need to repeatedly talk out her fears in psychoanalytic fashion.

Concerning the fictional character of Mrs. Reynolds, Stein writes, "The heroine is something I call a publicity saint—the modern saint being somebody who achieves publicity without having done anything in particular, everybody told me I could not do it, without making her do something, but, by God I did, and I am proud" (qtd. in Bonney 180). Although Mrs. Reynolds does not actually "do" anything that would constitute behavior to move the story along, she does make a conscious choice to endure war: "Do please said Mrs. Reynolds she said it to everybody do please be sure that the way to endure is to be really sure, yes said Mrs. Reynolds do please be sure" (212). Ultimately, the will to endure translates into an act of strength, and Stein emphasizes that Mrs. Reynolds, although sometimes fearful and occasionally despairing, remains a strong, female character in spite of war news and developments. She continues on with the business of living and managing her home front, bravely seeking news and deciding to remain at home rather than relocate to a safer location.

Similar to *Lifting Belly* and *Wars I Have Seen, Mrs. Reynolds* refutes logocentrism and embraces decentralizing tendencies; in other words, readers are treated to perspectives from the periphery of the traditional war narrative. *Mrs. Reynolds* positions women's experiences as important to accounts of war. The act of the main character relating her war experiences from an embodied female subject position (embodied because her corporeality and corporeal concerns influence her mind-set and inform her identity) on the home front destabilizes war narrative: female civilians can participate in the war effort, and women are shown to be affected by war as well. Moreover, the novel collapses what it means to be a soldier; in several instances Mrs. Reynolds is construed as a soldier on the home front by the third-person omniscient narrator. She talks with another soldier as a soldier in camaraderie, and a female friend tells her that a single woman is worth the equivalent of four soldiers. Like a soldier, Mrs. Reynolds displays courage and endures hardship. Although it is a novel set in the domestic economy, all of the events in *Mrs. Reynolds* are set against the backdrop of war, and the obsessive preoccupation with time and the birthdays of Angel Harper bespeak the themes and focus of the novel:[6] war and survival. The grand gesture of *Mrs. Reynolds* is the privileging of the survivor on the home front.

War is depicted in gendered terms by Stein as a gesture to the gendered division in traditional war narrative and responses to war. Mrs. Reynolds and Mr. Reynolds, for instance, have decidedly different views on war: "Men said Mrs. Reynolds always think they can make the whole world bigger but they can't said Mrs. Reynolds. Well they think they can said Mr. Reynolds. Yes but they cannot said Mrs. Reynolds" (140). It is significant that Mrs. Reynolds is given the last words in this passage; her point of view is thus privileged, and her protest of the war captures the sentiment of the novel as a whole. In her assumption of a gendered point of view Mrs. Reynolds faults men for war, specifically in trying to make the world bigger through colonialist and imperialist activity. Her perspective throughout the novel constitutes a single female response to war and provides an alternative view of the patriarchal pursuit. In most cases, however, Stein dismantles essentialist gender binaries instead of reaffirming them. In virtually all cases Mrs. Reynolds's point of view serves as a critique and a rebuttal, as it does with her denunciation of the already failed masculine project of expansion and acquisition (making one's national world bigger by expanding the number of colonial territories in national possession). What becomes clear as *Mrs. Reynolds* progresses is Stein's discernment of imbalances and her need to rewrite them to present a more well-rounded female characterization of Mrs. Reynolds.

Stein certainly explores and investigates gender politics in *Mrs. Reynolds*, but it is not a propagandistic novel. The deconstruction of gendered identities may be a liberal project, but Stein's views on government politics were anything but liberal. It is important to remember that Stein was profoundly conservative in her political views and lauded the Vichy official and German supporter Marshal Philippe Pétain,[7] whom she believed capable of holding France together (Whittier-Ferguson, "Stein in Time" 119). Stein and Toklas were protected by Bernard Faÿ, a Nazi collaborator who obtained from Pétain a guarantee of protection for Stein and her companion. Faÿ had previously translated *The Autobiography of Alice B. Toklas* into French and had been a friend of Stein's long before the outbreak of war. In fact, Stein had written a portrait of him in 1929. Zofia Lesinska nicely articulates the unhappy resonance of Stein's politics, resulting in critics' indignation with Stein and perhaps also contributing to the lack of scholarly interest in *Mrs. Reynolds*. According to Lesinska:

> It is difficult to condone the author's own insistence on living comfortably in the South of France under the auspices of Faÿ, a Vichyite and a resolute anti-Semite. While millions of people throughout Europe were humiliated and oppressed, Stein, despite being Jewish, was protected both as a friend of a prominent collaborationist and as an American national. Had she decided to leave her adopted country for the duration of the war, as a socially well-connected celebrity, she could have tried to secure American visas for her friends or strangers who fell victim to Nazi anti-Semitic terror in Europe.

> Perhaps she could have helped Max Jacob, a surrealist poet and a prewar frequenter of her salon, who, as a Jew, was arrested by the Gestapo and died in the Drancy concentration camp abandoned by friends. (317)

Consequently, many critics, understandably, are unwilling to let Stein's conservative politics off the hook. Unfortunately, however, Stein's response was not unusual: it is important to note that the majority of the French engaged in a "complicitous conformism" as a form of survival (Lesinska 317). This observation is certainly not meant to exonerate her; rather, it is to provide context. Stein, as a Jewish lesbian, had everything to lose, and she ultimately chose to stay silent in France (part of the protection bargain) as her and Toklas's best chance for survival. Stein admits to being "terribly frightened" in September 1939 by the impending war ("Winner" 615). It is also important to remember that Stein had lived in France for over thirty-five years by the time World War II broke out; she considered France her home.

Phoebe Stein Davis comments on Stein's "resistance": "She was contributing to, and helping, subversive new little magazines, vehicles used both to publish banned Jewish and homosexual writers and to circulate information about their whereabouts" (n. 5). Readers would also do well to remember that Stein denounces Hitler in *Mrs. Reynolds* and celebrates the Resistance in "The Winner Loses: A Picture of Occupied France." Linda Wagner-Martin concurs: "Her writing during the early war years—like her blatant title 'The Winner Loses'—clearly shows her sympathy with the French and her hatred of the Nazis" (243). Clearly, Stein did not support Nazi activity, but she remained oddly conservative, considering her identity, in her views on politics.

Ultimately, *Mrs. Reynolds* is neither a celebration of liberal nor conservative political views. Stein's avowal in the epilogue that *Mrs. Reynolds* is not concerned with historical accuracy but with the state of mind during "these years" situates the novel firmly within World War II while attempting to capture the psychological mind-set and bodily experience of a female civilian affected by the war (331). I contend that *Mrs. Reynolds* is very much a historical novel, although many critics have debunked its claims for historicity.[8] In fact, Stein herself once proclaimed, "History . . . really ought to come to be literature" (qtd. in Davis 574).

Interestingly, Stein dismisses the historical facticity of *Mrs. Reynolds* in her epilogue and implies that the novel is disassociated from time: "There is nothing historical about this book except the state of mind" (331). Maria Diedrich, however, reads the novel as grounded in historical factual reality. Readers may be able to "identify real historical events—from Hitler's Ruhr annexation, through the Munich agreement, to his assault on Poland and his defeat at Stalingrad, and eventually to the Allies' invasion of Italy and Normandy" (95). The supporting evidence is inferential rather than denotative. Although the Ruhr annexation is not specifically mentioned, Mrs. Reynolds fears her husband will be drafted.[9] In addition, although Moscow goes unnamed, invocations of Harper's anxiety over a red Russian moon underscore his anxiety concerning defeat.[10] References to a growing Resistance can also be discerned: "Just then Mrs. Reynolds heard a call and she went out and there in front of her door there were more and more, more soldiers and more soldiers . . . . she said well I am glad to see them" (248–49). The references to war activity are usually veiled and sometimes slight: "Just then an airplane flew over them, oh dear said Mrs. Reynolds and now you will be looking up and you will not tell me anything about what is going to happen." The implication from this passage is that something is certainly going to happen as a result of the Resistance, and Mrs. Reynolds speculates on the outcome: "Dear me said Mrs. Reynolds it is so tiresome not to know what is going to be happening, well anyway said Mrs. Reynolds perhaps Angel Harper is not going to have his fifty-second birthday or if he does perhaps he will not be a year older and if he is not then that will be the end of that" (246). I read *end of that* to mean the end of war; Mrs. Reynolds realizes the demise of Angel Harper will signify the end of World War II. Given this realization and the other veiled or coded historical incidents elaborated here, the novel is clearly grounded within a historical context.

The novel may seem to be irresponsibly disassociated from time and history because Stein refrains from identifying exactly where Mrs. Reynolds lives, even though geography and identity factor into war in important ways, as Stein was certainly aware. Her embodied situation as a Jewish, lesbian, American woman living in occupied France (marginalized on four counts: religion, sexuality, nationality, and gender) could have meant a very horrifying outcome for her and Toklas—if the other aspects of her situation had not rendered protection.[11] Her celebrity status as an American author in France may also have helped protect her. Stein relished her notoriety to some extent; in particular she appreciated the admiration from the American GIs because she admired them in turn. Her positive feelings about the United States and American soldiers play a part in defining Mrs. Reynolds's character.

In many of her other writings Stein reaffirms her American identity and is clearly proud of American troops. National affiliation is significant in times of war, and Stein is quite vocal about how American she is and how strong the United States is in the war. Likewise, Mrs. Reynolds even meditates on George Washington, and three stories Mr. Reynolds relates are American in content.[12] The Reynolds family shares Stein's enthusiasm for American militia and affairs in general. Stein's admiration of American GIs likely stems from an unconscious self-identification. She identifies herself as an American first and foremost, which she shares with the American soldiers, but she also sees herself as a veteran soldier in occupied France. The language used to describe Mrs. Reynolds supports this hypothesis: "Mrs. Reynolds liked to talk to John, they talked together as if they had been old soldiers. Well in a way they were, and that made them feel the same about things" (45). Mrs. Reynolds emerges as a war veteran in this passage, and we will see that Stein uses similar language to talk about herself in *Wars I Have Seen*. She seems to be saying here that simply surviving war, albeit in different circumstances, unites the (American) civilian and the (American) solider.

As Stein's advertising of her American affiliation and enthusiasm for American soldiers demonstrate, the novel is very much grounded in time, both in an awareness of time as passing and the acknowledgment that time in the historical setting of the novel has everything to do with the events alluded to and the reactions of Mrs. Reynolds throughout the text. Bridgman notes that, when Angel Harper turns fifty, his presence dominates the narrative, and if one takes into account Hitler's birth date of April 20, 1889, Harper's fiftieth birthday would place the novel in 1939, the year the war began (319). People die as a result of Harper's increasing age and power. Mr. Reynolds's cousin's family is presumed drowned, and Mrs. Reynolds attributes the news to the machinations of Angel Harper: "How could it not happen, Angel Harper was fifty years old and so it did happen" (182). Animals also become victims of the wartime situation when Angel Harper turns fifty, and their plight suggests situations in which people may find themselves: "And then said Mrs. Reynolds a lamb has died of hunger. What said Mr. Reynolds did I not tell you said Mrs. Reynolds the lamb of the Davilles' has died of hunger. Why said Mr. Reynolds did they not give it something to eat, because said Mrs. Reynolds they had nothing to feed it" (184). Stein's other works, such as *Wars I Have Seen,* portray her concern about food shortages and rationing because these deprivations were a very real part of her war experience. In *Mrs. Reynolds* Stein underscores the seriousness of war's impact on the home front for the Reynolds family specifically in terms of food shortage: "Oh said Mrs. Reynolds, if we all have less to eat we can get thin and tighten our belts, and if we have still less to eat and have to die of it then if we have to die of it we can all die together. Yes yes said Mr. Reynolds and it was true he said yes and he meant it, it might all come to be true as true as that" (89–90). Unlike *Lifting Belly,* the subject of death in connection to war surfaces many times in *Mrs. Reynolds.* This motif suggests that war may have wounded Mrs. Reynolds psychologically and emotionally, thus traumatizing her and requiring her to act out and process her trauma vocally.

The issue of death emerges in a somewhat complicated manner because of the peculiar tone Stein employs. The words in this passage clearly indicate anxiety, but, because Stein leaves out tonal markers, the tone cannot register in a superficial or profound manner. The understated tone of this passage correlates to the resignation of living with war threats every day. Stein continues to leave out tonal markers and to employ understatement when treating Angel Harper and his agenda: "Everybody said Mrs. Reynolds everybody hates Angel Harper and his fifty years, and she was right, she said she was right and she knew she was right, but it was not all right" (183). Angel Harper sets in motion a chain of events that are "not all right," and Mrs. Reynolds despises him for it; her condemnation of Angel Harper shows to what extent Mrs. Reynolds as a civilian is implicated in war dangers and knowledge. The understatement of "but it was not all right" enhances the direness of the fictional World War II situation. We know, from a twenty-first-century vantage point, how heinous the situation is, and Stein's use of understatement suggests to us, in ways that Stein could never have intended, that there is no language that can effectively capture the horror of Hitler's agenda in World War II. Thus, the use of understatement allows what cannot be successively articulated to remain unsaid. While understatement paradoxically underscores the importance of a situation, it also suggests the reluctance on Stein's part to delve into the characterization of the monstrous Hitler character; she attempts to distance herself from him in her fictional work. Mrs. Reynolds decides, for example, that there is no use in Angel Harper "having that name" (141). Sharing, perhaps, Mrs. Reynolds's concern with the potency of language, Stein thinly disguises the character of Hitler by giving him a different name: "Angel Harper, nobody likes to say Angel Harper and if they do like to say Angel Harper they do not say Angel Harper" (66). Stein does not call Hitler by his true name in *Mrs. Reynolds*, perhaps because she wishes to emphasize the fictional aspects of the novel or because she refuses to inscribe such a heinous person literally onto her text. At least with a proxy Stein can avoid the burden of responsible or faithful depictions.

But Stein does depict the dictator as ruminating on past formative incidents in his life. These episodes are almost couched as cautionary tales: the lesson learned pertains to deviance: performing outside of one's own gender constraints leads to dangerous consequences. Indeed, Angel Harper's childhood suggests "a lonely and disturbed development" (Bridgman 319). For the most part the narrator asserts that Angel Harper "never did cry" (54). At eight years old he is the target of a group of boys throwing stones; in this episode one hits him, and he cries. At nine he asks to have a prison built for him to sit in (276); at twelve he cross-dresses, wearing a girl's hat and his mother's apron, which makes for "a very strange costume" (279). Also at twelve, he refuses to use words that begin with the letter *f* (143). At fifteen Angel Harper constructs a seat at the base of a telegraph pole with a curtain and supervises his two large dolls, each in its own doll carriage (298). The episodes indicate telling, formative moments in the background of the instigator of "the most terrible war in the world" (47).

Overall, the young Angel Harper comes across as socially deviant: he wants to incarcerate himself seemingly because of his gender confusion and his unconventional behavior.

Stein suggests that the depravity of Angel Harper can be traced partly to his feelings of exclusion and powerlessness growing up. As a child, he was pelted with stones, and at fifteen he displays arrested development in playing with dolls. As Angel Harper ages, he increasingly thinks back to his childhood. In fact, the last memory introduced before Angel Harper is declared dead takes place when he is fourteen years old. His obsession with his childhood and adolescence becomes stronger as time progresses in the novel; he seems to become aware that certain events in his childhood were formative. Time markers, such as his birthdays, commemorate the memorable, often painful, moments upon which he ruminates. These moments give insight into Angel Harper's confused, gendered identity and his embodied experience. Because he does not fit in with the expectations of his gender, Angel Harper imprisons himself as a child and is stoned for misperforming. Consequently, under the rule of the adult Angel Harper, there is no room for misperformances; deviance becomes a liability, and punishment is meted out for deviants as well as for those who fall into an essentialist category deemed unacceptable by association with "acceptable" identities.

There seems to be a need on Stein's part to rationalize Angel Harper's evilness, and she explains it partly through examples of punishment and marginalization for deviant acts. In turn the dictator exacts vengeance on those who dare to deviate from convention. On the other hand, a positive aspect emerges from the retelling of the dictator's gender-bending and otherwise deviant behavior. His deviance, especially in connection with breaking gender conventions, puts into relief Mrs. Reynolds's own (although mild by contrast) "deviant" behavior. She thinks of herself in terms that do not resonate with her position because they are not culturally sanctioned. Mrs. Reynolds, for instance, assumes the identity of a soldier and the manager of her home, even though her husband continues to live with her during the war.

The passage of time in the novel is obsessively marked by Mrs. Reynolds's concern with and the dictator's own acknowledgment of his birthdays, but time is also heavily marked by domestic rituals. In Stein's domestic economy time is kept by regular domestic markers of activity. Going to bed is one such marker, and Mr. Reynolds is the advocate of bedtime. Retiring for the night is his solution to troublesome problems and anxiety. Sleep functions as an escape, but domestic rituals also add the comfort of routine. Liesl Olson reads Stein's preference for habit and routine as telling: "Habitual actions accumulate value and take precedence over the traumatic events of war. While one might assume that habits would be disrupted during a time of crisis (or substituted by an active reaction to war's violence) Stein's response to the Second World War was to keep her life as consistent and pleasurable as possible" (330). Stein personally found value in habitual behavior; reliance on habit indicates a desire for order, control, and comfort. If a routine during wartime attempts to establish normalcy and order amid change and chaos, habits could thus become a strategy for coping. Clearly, as Olson posits, habits during wartime "foreground habit's crucial utility," but that does not necessarily imply that the text emphasizes "habit's ultimate political inadequacy" (338). For Stein and for Mrs. Reynolds habits suit them as politically adequate: habits form a chosen response to a political situation. Because war is a political activity, coping with it, even on a personal level, becomes to some extent political, thus making habits personal and political responses to war within the domestic economy. Habits function, for example, as survival strategies for Mr. and Mrs. Reynolds. Generally following disturbing talk of Angel Harper or war, Mr. and Mrs. Reynolds retire: "It is not in beds that they will die said Mr. Reynolds and Mrs. Reynolds began to cry and then she stopped and said well said she what is there to say when everybody will be gone away. Mr. Reynolds said well I will go too, yes said Mrs. Reynolds I know but she was sure and it was true that it was not better so. Anyway not yet said Mrs. Reynolds anyway he that is Angel Harper is only forty-nine perhaps there will yet be time. Let us go to bed said Mr. Reynolds and they did so" (164–65). Going to bed becomes a coping strategy and a kind of survival tactic. Mr. and Mrs. Reynolds make a conscious choice to endure and strategize for survival, and their habits become personally political decisions when followed accordingly.

Time is also marked by the days of the week. In fact, the novel begins with a heavy marking of time by enumerating weekdays before giving way to Angel Harper's birthday as the dominant marker. As the beginning of the novel emphasizes, each day constitutes a milestone: "It really did make a difference, it is hard to believe that there is such a difference between Monday and Tuesday but there is. Anybody who has ever been through anything knows that" (19). Each passing day serves as a marker of survival. Measuring time in this way becomes something like the tracking of an accomplishment. In wartime "every day is another day when Angel Harper is forty-seven, even cake gets to have another meaning" (141). If a cake is a synecdoche for the domestic economy, then Stein is insisting on a reconfiguration of the domestic sphere during war. The domestic becomes redefined and understood in different terms.

John Whittier-Ferguson concurs: "When Stein writes about war, other differences become crucial as well—between private and public spheres, between past and present, between childhood and adulthood, between her own and others' points of view. Words themselves take on different meanings" ("Liberation" 406). The differences Whittier-Ferguson identifies indeed correlate to the redefining of the domestic: Stein draws attention to boundaries (I would also add gender roles—the differences between performances of male and female behavior) in order to deconstruct them by collapsing and conflating difference and normalcy. Thus, the influence of war is such that everything from ways to mark time to semantics is transformed. Indeed, the creative ways that Mrs. Reynolds tracks time (e.g., Angel Harper's birthdays) constitute structural organizing principles in the text. As a result, we have a female character organizing the structure of a war narrative within the confines of her home.

As dangerous as Angel Harper becomes, Mrs. Reynolds is strengthened by her faith in survival. The prophecies of Saint Odile are an important subtext in the novel.[13] The significance of the prophecies is twofold. First, they actually sustained Stein herself in war-torn Europe.[14] She found comfort and hope in them, a narrative for survival. In turn she imparts this strategy to Mrs. Reynolds, enabling her to be optimistic in times of despair. Oftentimes, Mrs. Reynolds is buoyed by her belief in Saint Odile and her prophecies: "Mrs. Reynolds said that if it were not for Saint Odile she could not have the courage to go on" (206). Even when she doubts or begins to lose faith in Saint Odile, these moments are short-lived and are replaced by a stronger faith in the veracity of the prophecies. The paramount importance of the prophecies of Saint Odile in *Mrs. Reynolds* is their symbolic representation as a survival narrative. Mrs. Reynolds also prays: "Mrs. Reynolds knew how to pray but she had not at that time any reason for prayer. Much later when Angel Harper had made everybody go to war and suffer Mrs. Reynolds every morning in her bath lying on her back and her hands pressed together prayed not against Angel Harper but she prayed for his opponent and she prayed against his friends" (47). Prayer, like the prophecies, correlates with the desire for tools to aid survival.

The second aspect of the prophecies that is significant is their function as an additional marker of time in the narrative. Structurally, the prophecies are important to the text. They order disparate elements through the recurring allusions to Saint Odile and her prophecies. Indeed, allusions to Saint Odile occur more than any others, with the obvious exception of references to Hitler. As a result of the structural principle of the prophecies, the text is given a sort of coherence that would not otherwise be achieved. In short the prophecies of Saint Odile work to effect a narrative of survival that is both content and form driven. It would have been very unlike Stein and unusual of her work if she had not infused the form of *Mrs. Reynolds* with structural principles informed by the issues and concerns addressed in the content. Stein remarked in 1935: "The great thing is never to think about form but let it come. But does that sound strange from me? They have accused me of thinking of nothing else. Do you see the real joke? It is the critics who have really thought about form always and I have thought about—writing!" (qtd. in Miller 81). Narratives of time, illustrated in the retelling of prophecies, function as strategies used to impose order on wartime chaos, and the structural devices in the novel model this desire for order over chaos.

And war is chaotic; it is depicted as an uncontained enterprise in *Mrs. Reynolds*. Because it is dangerously unconfined, it can appear anywhere at any time, which heightens the anxiety of the characters. Hence, a sort of boundlessness and liminality are assigned to war in the novel, which may explain the lack of identifiable locations: "Where should they live, well they might live anywhere as when and since Angel Harper was forty-nine sooner or later they would have to go away. Mrs. Reynolds said when she met them how do you do are you still here, and they were" (163). Voluntary relocation was a strategy to avoid war dangers, but no one knows exactly when to relocate, as Mrs. Reynolds intimates in her queries to her interlocutor about unrealized travel plans. In fact, Mrs. Reynolds herself apparently considers relocation in this passage, but she never does, although she dreads invasion. It is, of course, never specified where exactly the Reynolds family lives, even though the details in *Mrs. Reynolds* corroborate Stein's own state of mind as detailed in *Wars I Have Seen*—and so we can make inferences. Mrs. Reynolds and Mr. Reynolds might fear invasion, but we have no idea how likely such an invasion might be.

Regardless of the precise location of Mr. and Mrs. Reynolds, we are told that they dismiss the advice and example of their acquaintances concerning exile or relocation, just as Stein and Toklas do in *Wars I Have Seen*. Ultimately, neither Stein nor Mrs. Reynolds is put in a desperate position. The threat of bodily harm is kept at bay. Yet psychological fear remains a part of Mrs. Reynolds's life after she decides against relocation, and her courage in what she perceives as a dangerous or potentially dangerous situation is remarkable (and unwise). Much like Stein, Mrs. Reynolds sees the war out without escaping to another country: "She knew she said it too she knew that staying where you were was something but never going away that was something too, and she was not sure, and she knew that going away all the time going on going away was something and not having any place to stay was something. Naturally she never said anything about this something because if she did well she would change it to something else that was the only way not to be frightened all day and as a matter of fact and it was true, Mrs. Reynolds was really not frightened at all not at all frightened" (207). Her resolve "not [to be] frightened" does not make her immune to fear. Indeed, the assertion that Mrs. Reynolds was not frightened in the least suggests that the unreliable narrator of *Mrs. Reynolds* is not entirely forthcoming and even mistaken: there is too much protestation, and the last line belies fear. In fact, in various passages of the novel Mrs. Reynolds understandably cries as a result of being afraid, but her resolve to persevere and carry out the daily, domestic tasks, such as foraging for food, is courageous.

Home becomes an unfamiliar place for Mrs. Reynolds because of war: "All this time Mrs. Reynolds was ready to come home. She and Mr. Reyn-

olds had not been away but she was ready to come home" (130). Mrs. Reynolds desires the war to end so that home can regain its status as a haven of refuge and safety. She is eager for the reimposition of some boundaries, the boundaries war has dissolved in regard to home as a safe haven: in this instance, Mrs. Reynolds wants *home* to mean "home" in familiar ways. She is not interested in dismantling the comforts of home, but the concept of home is profoundly altered during wartime.

Home does not designate a safe haven due to the uncontained nature of war. Angel Harper's war encroaches upon the safety of everyone, and this type of transgression is protested in the novel. The larger-than-life figures of Angel Harper and Joseph Lane are metaphorically everywhere, as their shadows affirm, and so they transcend geographical place and space. Although neither of these men ever physically meets Mrs. Reynolds, their presence and their lives impact hers. Harper's continual presence and influence causes Mrs. Reynolds to note "a dark cloud, a very dark one," and to dub it metaphorically an "Angel Harper cloud" (90). His willingness to transgress geographical borders (read: boundaries) endangers Mrs. Reynolds. His presence is omnipresent, and Mrs. Reynolds cannot refrain from discussing Angel Harper in detail and occasionally mentioning the undeveloped character of Joseph Lane because their decisions impact her life.

The palpable presence of Angel Harper causes Mrs. Reynolds to seek out interlocutors. Language, in fact, constitutes a potential means of therapy in *Mrs. Reynolds*. The experience of war is such that Mrs. Reynolds often feels a need to talk over matters in a psychoanalytic way, in the same vein as Freud's "taking cure." For her expressing the trauma of war through language becomes a therapeutic outlet. Indeed, Mrs. Reynolds, like Stein in *Wars I Have Seen*, actively seeks out passersby for news and solicits them for conversation and companionship. Talk forges a connection between her and other human beings, which combats the disconnectedness and disruption of war. Because of the war, many of Mrs. Reynolds's friends and acquaintances are no longer in regular communication. Transportation, other than walking, is hard to come by, and many have fled to what they perceive as safer places: "In a little while everybody ran" (61). Even Mrs. Reynolds's brother-in-law, William, and his wife, Hope, figure less prominently once war breaks out than they do initially in the novel. These conditions drastically alter the quality of Mrs. Reynolds's civilian life. But talking appears to have a cathartic effect on the main character. As a metanarrative, *Mrs. Reynolds* allows Stein the opportunity to address the emotional and psychological upheavals of the war years from a female perspective.

Mrs. Reynolds is not always forthcoming, however, about her feelings and experiences of war. At one point she wants to separate her home life from worries about the war. Silence becomes her tactic to extricate herself from the burden of war-related concerns, but her attempts at silence fail to distance her from the current worries and problems. For a time Mrs. Reynolds refuses to hear Angel Harper's name spoken or listen to talk of the war, believing in the power of language to such an extent that she assigns it almost omnipotent power. The importance of naming and articulation is given credence by Stein in Mrs. Reynolds's nightmarish dream that suggests the anonymity of mass killing:

> Once upon a time Mrs. Reynolds, she was dreaming this of course once upon a time Mrs. Reynolds began to think that everything was extra. Whatever she had was extra, not regular but extra, even Mr. Reynolds was extra and as she was thinking that everything was extra she suddenly turned and as she turned she saw somebody come in. And as he came in she said to herself what is his name and then she woke up, and that frightened her not the waking up but that nobody had a name and she told Mr. Reynolds her dream and he said perhaps it will come to that that nobody will have a name and Mrs. Reynolds said she would not like that at all, and Mr. Reynolds said her liking it or not would not stop it. And she knew he was right it would not. (189)

This passage denotes both the fear of mass killings and the fear of this type of violence actually occurring, as Mr. Reynolds dryly remarks: "Mr. Reynolds said her liking it or not would not stop it." The fairy tale beginning of this passage, "once upon a time," contrasts with the nightmarish quality of Mrs. Reynolds's dream. The expectations set up by "once upon a time" are thwarted by the horrific implications that human life is dispensable: Mr. Reynolds may be counted in a future death toll in this dangerous political climate. The last sentence in particular rings with a sense of foreboding: "And she knew he was right it would not." Unfortunately, as we know, the terror Mrs. Reynolds feels is prompted by and corresponds to very real mass killings. Throughout *Mrs. Reynolds* the events intimated and dramatized are poised as responses to the actual political climate and trauma of World War II. This scene also comments on the foreclosure of women's responses to war in general. Her opinions in this instance do not matter much to Mr. Reynolds; he subtly dismisses her commentary, and she ends up agreeing with him.

Mrs. Reynolds's ability to witness the everyday reality of war and the emotional experience of life on the home front is conducive to creating the mental state produced in the novel. The novel is extremely repetitive, detailing the mundane and the quotidian. And yet part of the ordinary experience of civilian life for Mrs. Reynolds is a fear of bodily harm. The novel dismantles not only the idea of home as a safe place but also the female body as a safe container/place. "She knew when people were dangerous, dangerous to themselves and dangerous to anybody dangerous to life and limb. She liked to say life and limb and she knew that when Angel Harper was really forty-nine that it was not really that, it was not that he was dangerous to life and limb, but life and limb, oh dear life and limb and Mrs. Reynolds knew and she said it too there was too much to say to do anything, oh dear she said life and limb, and she just did say that thing she just did say life and limb" (159). The focus here is certainly on the activity of war, the goal of overpowering the enemy through destruction of "life and limb" for a victory. Mrs. Reynolds's trauma manifests itself in her repeated concern over bodily injury. In no other place in the novel do we get such a condensed passage exhibiting sheer fear over injury: the body itself, suggested by the synecdoche of limb, is invoked no less than seven times in two Steinian sentences. At one point in the passage Mrs. Reynolds avers that "there was too much to say to do anything," but all she can articulate is the phrase *life and limb* over and over, as if she is acting out her trauma.

Fear and anxiety constitute the overriding tones of this passage and suggest war-related psychological or emotional wounding (i.e., trauma)—and for good reason. War, in its most basic form, is destructive. According to Elaine Scarry in *The Body in Pain: The Making and Unmaking of the World,*

"The main purpose and outcome of war is injuring" (63). The paradigmatic experience of war is that which is dictated by its structure—injured individuals. Mrs. Reynolds blames Angel Harper for the threat of injury, and she intuits what Scarry clarifies: the business of war is inflicting harm on bodies.

Scarry argues that the structure of war needs to be recognized for what it truly is, the systematization of destructive force, but war rhetoric in general elides injury and displaces it from the conversation. One can read many accounts of war "without encountering the acknowledgment that the purpose of the event is to alter the surface (to burn, to blast, to shell, to cut) human tissue, as well as to alter the surface, shape, and deep entirety of objects that human beings recognize as an extension of themselves" (Scarry 64). The domestic objects and activities of home function as necessary extensions of the people who live there. So it is to be expected that home life will subsequently change as war becomes widespread and domestic boundaries become transgressed: "One at a time never happens with bombs said Mr. Reynolds' younger brother William, it is always two at a time, and said Hope his wife I do not like hare to be too far gone before they cook it" (102). Foregrounding the chaotic blurring of boundaries that accompanies war, William's observation about bombing is directly connected to Hope's preference in food preparation. The traditionally masculine political outside world is juxtaposed with the domestic interior world of women. The conjunction *and* bespeaks linkage: bombing and domestic affairs are not mutually exclusive. Instead, bombing, itself the image par excellence of a blowing apart of boundaries, infiltrates the domestic sphere, causing a rupture of boundaries between the binary construction of the male world of war and the female domestic space of home, and in the process distinctions between public and private, unsafe and safe, exterior and interior, and masculine and feminine are unsettled.

Elsewhere in the novel, a shortage of eggs and the scarcity of stockings and gloves signify the extent to which war has interfered with civilians' domestic business.[15] Maintaining the business of home, the domestic economy, is a difficult task, one in which "they cannot cook for the day after tomorrow" or take care of other tasks in advance because "there was nothing to buy and it all costs so much money" (245, 262). Yet, as managers of the home and the home front economy, women perform work that men cannot: "And so said Mrs. Reynolds women think they can do something when men cannot do it, some women feel like that said Mrs. Reynolds and then they act" (245). The notion of women as active contributors values the work of women in the domestic, home front economies during wartime.

Stein highlights this point: "Mrs. Reynolds said even if I am sleepy I do want to know about civilians being dead. Civilians said Mrs. Reynolds, I met a girl today her name was Ruth and I asked her just what you asked me and she said, one woman makes four soldiers, so what is a civilian and I said what is a civilian and now you ask me what is a civilian" (280). In case her privileging of women's courage, survival tactics, and wartime contributions went unheeded, here Stein spells out for the reader one of the messages of *Mrs. Reynolds:* the semantics and values of war and wartime need to be revised to include the female civilian as a principal participant and contributor. Stein employs hyperbole—one woman is worth four soldiers—to make Ruth's point that woman are significant players in wartime. The question of what defines a civilian is posed three times with the implication that the term *soldier* needs further consideration and with the result that definitions of *soldier* are evacuated in this passage. Ruth is given authority in the text; her claim is uncontested by Mrs. Reynolds or Stein. As such, Stein bestows authority on Ruth, which lends credibility to Ruth's assertion that women deserve acknowledgment of their suffering, bravery, and contributions—and, more generally, their presence in wartime.

The language of the novel mirrors the mental states during war of noncombatants, the authorial artistic intention of *Mrs. Reynolds* as stated in the epilogue. The repetitive and singsong quality of the language underscores the mundane quality of day-to-day life, living with war day after day is tiresome, but war is reluctantly accepted as a part of daily life by Mrs. Reynolds and others on the home front. In this way war becomes domesticated. Each day is the same as the last, with another day yet to survive through and nothing seeming to change. Stein also uses repetitive and singsong language to capture this very feeling in *Wars I Have Seen:* "Tired of winter tired of war but anyway they do hope and pray that it will end some day" (150). The singsong language resembles the language used in nursery rhymes; essentially, it is domestic language converted into language to talk about war. "There was no use in insisting said Mrs. Reynolds but if I did wish said Mrs. Reynolds I would wish that Angel Harper would break a dish. A dish of what said Mr. Reynolds. A dish which would make him late. Late for what said Mr. Reynolds late for being forty-eight, said Mrs. Reynolds and they both laughed a little and as it was late they said it was so late that they would go to bed and they did" (144–45). Consequently, Stein opens up a new way to address war. The singsong language is free of clichés and, in Steinian fashion, revitalizes war discourse. The incongruous marriage of content (war) and form (reminiscent of nursery rhymes) is unsettling and indicates corruption.[16] Dickie suggests that rhyme in Stein's war writings points to artifice and to the reification of textual boundaries (45). War is something that is artificially constructed, and rhyme may simply be a tool to scaffold artificiality or acknowledge the limitations of a text to represent the massive chaos that is the very nature of war. On the other hand, such linking of content and form suggests that the corruption of war has utterly permeated the domestic arena, and there are no (textual) boundaries left. But the invocation of nursery rhyme–like language can also serve as retreat from the brutal language that should rightly communicate the horrors of war. The comical language provides relief while simultaneously underscoring fear or horror.

Carolyn Faunce Copeland observes that "the rhyming not only makes the fixed historical identity of Angel Harper irrelevant, problematic, and weirdly human, but it also undermines or ignores the weight of history as a matter of frozen record: 'A cold moon that came up not too soon but not at noon.' The phrase strips the weight from the historical event, but in some ways it encircles the *nature* of the historical fact that Hitler was defeated by the Russians" (166). This explication accords with the design of *Mrs. Reynolds* as a whole: the entire narrative references history and personal experience, but it is an unfixed, problematic, and sometimes irrelevant record of life lived. For these reasons *Mrs. Reynolds* may be the epitome of Stein's prose experimentation. Lloyd Frankenburg, in his foreword to the Yale edition of *Mrs. Reynolds*, notes: "In many ways *Mrs. Reynolds* is the culmination of Gertrude Stein's narrative style. This might be called a style by repetition, transposition, and accretion; to which must be added omission. Rather than developing by means of a beginning, a middle, and an end, its effect is one of endlessness" (xii). The play of language (the rhyming and nursery rhyme quality of it) works in tandem with the structure of the novel (a narrative of "endlessness" that constitutes a catalogue of responses to mundane events) to create a new type of experimental war novel that insists on women's presence in war narrative without mimicking traditional war histories or male narratives.

As difficult and obscure as *Mrs. Reynolds* is, it is perhaps unsurprising that the criticism is very sparse. At the moment it is certainly not the most widely read of Stein's works, and it is fortunate and somewhat surprising that the work was recently in print—until Sun and Moon Press folded in 2004. I suspect that the physical act of reading the novel may constitute the primary deterrent. The experience of reading *Mrs. Reynolds* provides the reader with the same feelings of monotony and confusion that the characters in the novel harbor, at the expense of the reader's pleasure: "Gertrude Stein's most intricate reaction to those years [life in the French provinces in the early years of World War II] was *Mrs. Reynolds,* a long novel in which she reverted to the monotonous discontinuities and obscurity of her earlier career. *Mrs. Reynolds* cannot be advanced as a pleasurable reading experience. Its record of pointless and apparently repetitive experiences is often irritating" (Bridgman 318). Bridgman's dismissal of *Mrs. Reynolds* is harsh; the novel may not constitute a pleasurable reading experience, but it is certainly not "pointless." Similar to *Lifting Belly, Mrs. Reynolds* is experiential; autobiographical tidbits can be identified, and readers are invited to experience the mind-set of a female civilian during wartime. This experiential quality helps to authenticate the agenda of the work, as Stein defines it in the epilogue: "This book is an effort to show the way anybody could feel these years" (331). *Mrs. Reynolds* privileges the female survivor, all the while intimating civilian hardships and detailing the mind-set of a female character.

In her last and arguably most experimental novel Stein creates a narrative that resembles poetry in its stylistic techniques of language, the "formal heightening or stylization" of "language art" (DeKoven, *Rich and Strange* 187–88). Furthermore, in its "unmediated" anti-referentiality, a characteristic DeKoven assigns to poetry, and its perhaps unintentional foregrounding of form, *Mrs. Reynolds* is closer to poetry than prose. As a result, Stein produces an experimental war novel from a female perspective, one that appropriately blurs generic boundaries on many levels in her investigation of gendered identity and war. Stein delivers a feminist response to war in *Mrs. Reynolds* that erodes the distinctions and boundaries linking and designating genres, identities, and patriarchal war narrative. The major, physical battles of the war are left uncharted and are only intimated. The quotidian, domestic battles are privileged instead. I maintain that this novel *is* a Steinian response to war: Mrs. Reynolds is an integrated and embodied character in the sense that her lived experience, corporeal concerns, and mind-set are foregrounded in a novel set in wartime. The character of Mrs. Reynolds and her experiences are informed by Stein's embodiment, as we will see in *Wars I Have Seen.*

Wars I Have Seen and Stein's World War II Experiences

The long, autobiographical *Wars I Have Seen,* published in 1945, constitutes Stein's lengthiest account of civilian life during war. It is a tedious day-to-day reflection upon Stein's life and interests during the occupation and the first days of liberation. Like *Mrs. Reynolds,* nothing much happens in terms of a plot, but *Wars I Have Seen* amplifies the experiential discussion of war found in *Mrs. Reynolds* from a female perspective and authenticates the "historical . . . state of mind" that Stein claims to reproduce in the epilogue of *Mrs. Reynolds* (331). The monotony and hardships of civilian life are replicated and enumerated, but what is significant about *Wars I Have Seen* is its unabashed and unwavering focus on one woman's life on the home front during war. Stein, like Mrs. Reynolds, compares herself to a soldier, lumping herself into the same category as the war veteran she converses with in her autobiography: "Well as I was saying I was talking to Monsieur Gallais, he had fought the last war the 1914 war, of course everybody of that age in France did, and we were telling each other stories as veterans do about how sweet everybody had been then" (150–51). As this statement attests, Stein thinks of herself as a war veteran, which may explain her fascination with American soldiers in *Wars I Have Seen* and *Brewsie and Willie* (1946).

Elsewhere in *Wars,* Stein presumes upon her status when conversing with another veteran. Toward the end of the war she comes upon a Maquis, a French underground resistance fighter, in a taxi. Like the other French townspeople, Stein esteems and celebrates the Maquis for their bravery. She and Toklas are "delighted" that the Maquis is wearing the French tricolor and looks so "bronzed and capable." She immediately introduces herself as an American, presuming an equal status with the Maquis and thus a favorable reception with him, which she receives: "We solemnly shook hands and congratulated each other" (233). The hyperbolic seriousness ("solemnly shook hands," "congratulated each other") with which Stein treats this scene is humorous, although Stein surely did not intend to be funny while asserting her own authority and importance in her war diary. One is left to wonder why it is exactly the Maquis is congratulating Stein, and yet she deigns not to clarify it because, in her mind, no explanation is necessary: she has survived a war too. This scene with the Maquis reaffirms Stein's status as a credible war narrator. We learn from Stein that the resistance fighter is, in fact, a captain of the Maquis, and he has, moreover, been a prisoner in Germany. Depicting a scene in which a war hero offers her respect, Stein aims to convince the reader that her war experience and knowledge are valuable.

The quotidian treatment of war is the theme that carries through the majority of Stein's war writings because her focus, during World War II especially, was helping Toklas manage the home. In *Wars I Have Seen* Stein explains, "I suppose there comes the saturation point of worry and then normal life begins again and just goes on being" (120–21). At some point, Stein says, life adjusts to what becomes "normal" in wartime. She emphasizes the mundane in daily life in her autobiographical writing, just as she does in her fictional work. Although *Mrs. Reynolds* seems to be about nothing more than a minute recording of Mrs. Reynolds's recurring worries and the execution of seemingly insignificant tasks such as securing food and news, these aspects are significant in that they are faithful to Stein's own experience of war, as evidenced in *Wars I Have Seen*. Stein explains: "And so many people are afraid and some cry all the time but most of the French people just go on taking trains and traveling about and really do not stop to bother about anything except how to get something extra to eat. We all do, we all keep on doing it, and everybody does it and now nobody really pays any attention to it" (183). While identifying herself throughout this text as, first and foremost, an American, Stein exudes pride over the French way of dealing with life in wartime and adopts that strategy. As a result, much of her World War II autobiography focuses on food: identifying available types of food, securing food, transporting food, and thinking about food in general.

On a single page, for instance, Stein alternates her discussion between food availability and ruminations of what she has eaten that day: "God bless chickens eggs are so nice, I had a fresh egg to-day, to be sure meat besides and potatoes and carrots and apples, so we are not suffering for food, but the poor people even the rich ones in the big cities, it is very bad" (177). Earlier Stein enumerates the tasks one performs in tending to hens and calculates how many eggs there will be, before breaking into a digression on the behavior of dogs and returning to the topic of eggs and chickens. In one way or another food is constantly on Stein's mind in *Wars I Have Seen:* "It is a queer life one leads in a modern war, every day so much can happen and every day is just the same and is mostly food, food and in spite of all that is happening every day is food" (12). In *Mrs. Reynolds* we saw the main character's concern with food and food shortages.[17] Clearly, Mrs. Reynolds's situation and embodiment are informed by Stein's actual war situation and her embodiment—namely, her corporeal concerns and mind-set about such fundamental needs as food.

Contemporary reviews by Carl Van Vechten, a close friend of Stein and the editor of her *Selected Writings*, and Djuna Barnes showcase the achievements and the shortcomings of *Wars I Have Seen.* Van Vechten has nothing but praise for Stein in a letter dated March 1945: "I have been reading Wars I Have Seen [*sic*]. . . . It is an amazing book in which you have imprisoned your feeling about all the world in the microcosm of a small French village. Never has your 'style' been so wedded to your subject matter or to the effect you planned to make on your reader" (qtd. in Burns 767). For Van Vechten, Stein accomplishes in her war journal what she set out to do in *Mrs. Reynolds:* she encapsulates her war response, her emotional state of mind, in the voice and body of a female civilian. Life during war is meted out in day-by-day accounts, rendered in excruciating detail in a sometimes labored style. In the majority of Stein's war texts the style tends toward the monotonous, the verbose, and sometimes the difficult and obscure. Stein writes, for example, of the German soldiers in April 1944, "When you are weak and brutal you are very much more hated than when you are strong and brutal, that is natural enough and that is what is happening now, nobody says of them now all the same they are still strong, and so although I am not sure that they are any more brutal than they were their not being strong any more and just as brutal makes them more hated than they ever were before" (170). Without standard punctuation and with the use of a double negative and repeated words in this single sentence, the nuances of Stein's meaning must be teased out. She appears to be mirroring the confused and difficult state of affairs with her confusing syntax choices: the Germans are getting weaker as a military unit, but they are still brutal as individuals. What Stein makes clear in this awkwardly constructed passage is the French hatred of the brutal German soldiers; they are disliked more in April 1944 than ever before by the French people, and this passage, despite its purposeful complexity, propounds these sentiments.

Additionally, as Van Vechten indicates in his review, the prolix style that Stein favors, along with the pervasive use of repetition, re-creates the tediousness Stein's characters assign to the quality of life during war. The scarcity of clothes, for example, is underscored by the repetition of a tedious activity: "Everybody is so tired of darning everything, that is of course Alice Toklas who does all the darning, and darning darns and then darning the darned darns everybody is getting tired of darning everything, everybody is" (188). By the end of this Steinian sentence we are almost as tired of darning as Alice Toklas is of it. And yet Stein manages to emphasize the scarcity of supplies, which constitutes a privation, while foregrounding women's work during war. Although Toklas is engaged in domestic work, her work is still valued as important (and thus worthy of mention), albeit tedious.

The tedium of living in occupied France clearly emerges in Stein's refusal to be friendly with a German soldier who tries to ingratiate himself with the French in May 1944, when the French were becoming confident that the Germans would be defeated: "In the meantime there are Germans here in the railroad station as station masters and one of them the one that is always hoping that everybody will be nice to him after the German defeat because he has always been very nice, now comes in to the park here of the property to rest himself, it is a nuisance we do not know how to get rid of him, he wants to be friendly but of course we do not, of course we do not, certainly of course we do not. And so we do not forget to remember that they are here, very little just here but still always ever here" (179). Stein notes her frustration with the "nuisance" of German occupation in France and underscores her annoyance through the reiteration of her displeasure with the "friendly" German four successive times. And she ensures that her reader will also "remember that they are here" because, until the very end of *Wars I Have Seen,* we are reminded that the Germans are "still always ever here." In fact, Stein keeps track of the number of soldiers stationed in Culoz, where she lives, and repeatedly divulges the number for the reader. The number matters to her because it signifies changes in war strategy and German strength.

The tally is a very real concern that occupies Stein's everyday thoughts. She offers an account of July 1944: "As a matter of fact the forty-odd Germans who are here and who no longer get their pay are getting more and more peaceful, they ask for work they wander around unarmed and they used never to stir without a gun on their back and never less than three together, now they wander all about the country alone and unarmed." Again, Stein emphasizes the prevalence of Germans in her town and the beginning of the end of occupation as observed through changes in attitude and behavior. In the next paragraph Stein relies on repetition to show that, while the Germans are wreaking havoc, they are still an oppressive presence, and the recurring allusions in the text become burdensome to the reader as well. Although Stein has just mentioned the soldier count in the preceding paragraph, she mentions it again: "We still have forty odd and when will they leave very soon we are hoping, they do not do anything very disagreeable here but oh dear what a relief it will be when they are gone, as everybody says even when they are not doing anything they are an oppressive burden, they are" (208–9). These examples illustrate the uses of repetition: repetition captures the monotonous quality of civilian life, Stein's—and the French people's—adamant dislike of German soldiers during occupation, and the almost hysteric concern over the quotidian details of civilian life, belying Stein's dislike of war's intrusion on civilian life and her fear of potential dangers.

Djuna Barnes reviews *Wars I Have Seen* in the June 1945 edition of *Contemporary Jewish Record.* She finds it surprisingly sentimental, naive, and bordering on the brink of originality:

> Thrown off by the "happy idiot" simplifications, the baby-like repetition, I am come to the conclusion that, in spite of its place and time in history, and willingly acknowledging its many acute observations, the very thing which her devotees praise, though they would be the first to deny it, is her flowing sentimentality.
>
> . . . .
>
> You do not feel that she is ever really worried about the sorrows of the people; her concern at its highest pitch is a well-fed apprehension. She says well-fed people—that is, people who love their food as the French do—never lose wars; the Germans lose wars because their food is awful.
>
> . . . .
>
> I should like to keep the book, but she always takes her writing away. (136–38)

Having both lived in France and written about war herself, Barnes's interest in reviewing Stein's war autobiography reflects similarities in her own background. Astutely, Barnes intuits that Stein is part of a larger project, one that encompasses her as well, of writing women into war narrative and representing women in connection to war experience and war history. As a result, she acknowledges that Stein is saying something interesting to her: "I should like to keep the book, but she always takes her writing away." Barnes faults Stein for stopping short of a primer for women's war writing, in spite of the fact that Stein offers a more direct, basic, and personal account of war than Barnes. What Stein gives readers instead, Barnes contends, is a naive and sentimental account of civilian life in France. Barnes refrains from condemning Stein's sentimentalism, but she points it out as the most attractive quality to Stein's devotees.

Like Barnes herself and H.D., Stein locates military conflict within the domestic economy and alludes to war experience on the home front to insist on women's presence during war and to expound upon women's (sometimes real and sometimes imagined) experiences of it. Such literary representations, grounded as they are in woman-centered issues (the home, the female body, emotional response), gesture to the sentimental literature produced by women in the nineteenth century. Each of the authors in this study owes some literary debt to sentimentalism. Thus, Barnes's major point of contention with Stein is not her sentimentalism but her seemingly childish innocence. Faulting Stein for harboring only "well-fed apprehension" and for espousing such naive illogic as "Germans lose wars because their food is awful," Barnes implies that Stein's response to military conflict in *Wars I Have Seen* is glib; it precludes her from worrying about "the sorrows of her people." The major fault of Stein's writing, for Barnes, is Stein's presumed or assumed naïveté.

I suspect that Stein's naïveté is an assumed tone, but readers such as Barnes presume that Stein must really be exceptionally unwary. She certainly does come across in many instances as an uncritical war participant and war chronicler, glibly writing at one point: "Anyway financially there is no sense in anti-semitism. That is what I say" (56). Beginning the sentence with *Anyway* makes the sentence an afterthought, rather than the main point of the paragraph. Furthermore, this sentence is tacked on at the very end of the paragraph, which contributes to the sense of it as flippant. Her declaration that anti-Semitism makes no sense financially to her, transforming her claim into a personal opinion, further detracts from the seriousness of Jewish persecution. Although she was advised to leave France in order to avoid detention in a concentration camp, Stein off-handedly remarks that "Oscar Wilde and the Ballad of Reading Gaol was the first thing that made me realize that it could happen, being in prison" (55). These types of remarks undercut the reader's confidence in Stein as a discerning and politically cognizant war reporter. Stein seems unaware of the dangerous situation for people with identities that were considered liabilities: "Oh well these days nobody minds death from fear of heaven or hell but there is there always is with death the cessation of life and life is interesting, and certainly it is for Hitler so why stop" (231). No judgment is passed on Hitler by Stein, and her cryptic "why stop" could be a glib reference to herself (she should continue living and writing while life is interesting) or to Hitler (he should continue his activities if he finds them so interesting). Elsewhere Stein's treatment of the German occupation in France is almost one of abated excitement; there is no trace of an understanding of the dangers a German encampment brings to the town: "Here we are in the heart of the French country with near a hundred German soldiers right in this village and wire entanglements and little block houses all around the railway station and it is exactly like a novel or a theatre" (187). Yet Stein explains her dismissive attitude toward war danger: "Well this time [World War II] the French . . . could only suffer the nervousness and anxiety of wars, they were not in it, that is to say of course now they are in it but from '40 to '43 well really into the beginning of '44 they were not in it, they had all the nervousness the anxiety and the suffering and privations of war but they were not in it" (213). *Mrs. Reynolds* was written from 1940 to 1943, during the window in which France was suffering "the nervousness and anxiety" of war but was "not in it." *Wars I Have Seen* is able to complete the picture of Stein's experience of World War II. In both works Stein (and Mrs. Reynolds) appears strangely removed from war in many ways. Her observation that France was "not in it" until 1944 to some extent justifies her disinterest and naive attitude concerning war threats.

Some readers have assumed that Stein is a naive war chronicler because of her lack of seriousness in relation to war matters, but Stein certainly knows more than her pose suggests. Throughout *Wars I Have Seen* Stein gives us hints that she is much more aware of the political climate and the dangerousness of her situation than Barnes gives her credit for or than might otherwise be expected from her light treatments of war matters. Early on in her war autobiography, Stein relates how her lawyer tried to persuade her and Toklas to leave for Switzerland immediately at the behest of the former *sous préfet* at Belley. According to Stein, her lawyer recalls, "Maurice Sivain said to me, tell these ladies that they must leave at once for Switzerland, to-morrow if possible otherwise they will be put into a concentration camp" (50). Stein and Toklas elected to stay in their adopted country, but Stein expresses uneasiness at the prospect of concentration camps (or otherwise being forcibly removed) and relocation: "It is disconcerting to know and it gives you a funny feeling, that any time not only that you can be told to go and you go but also that you can be taken. Nevertheless you stay, and if you stay you do not go away" (27). Her uneasiness bespeaks her limited knowledge of war crimes and perhaps explains her reticence on the topic of persecution.

There are, however, two chilling descriptions of war activity. The first suggests a concentration camp roundup: "They [Italians or French who have been taken to work in Germany] usually go in ordinary passenger trains but these were going into freight cars and that usually is only done with soldiers . . . and so it did look rather sad, and they told us they were young men and girls that had been rounded up in Annecy and were being taken well somewhere, did they have any reason for being taken, well probably and where were they being taken nobody ever does know and every day is another day" (172–73). Because of the unusual nature of the roundup (civilian passengers loaded into freight cars, the sad appearance of the scene, various people rounded up for unknown reasons and headed to an unknown destination), it is possible that Stein witnessed a war crime. She is obviously uncomfortable teasing out the implications of the roundup and abruptly changes the subject.

It may be that Stein is simply ignorant of the particulars of the political situation and prefers to remain so. And yet the second scene, which comes at the end of the book, demonstrates Stein's (at least partial) knowledge of war crime and persecution:

> They [Americans in France] used all of them to want to know how we managed to escape the Germans and gradually with their asking and with the news that in the month of August the Gestapo has been in my apartment in Paris to look at everything, naturally I began to have what you might call a posthumous fear. I was quite frightened. All the time the Germans were here [in Culoz] we were so busy trying to live through each day that except once in a while when something happened you did not know about being frightened, but now somehow with the American soldiers questions and *hearing what had been happening to others, of course one knew it but now one had time to feel it* and so I was quite frightened, now that there was nothing dangerous. (255; emph. added)

Here Stein admits to knowing something of the persecution of Jews ("of course one knew it") but being unable to register it while living in the midst of occupation. She suffers a "posthumous" fear, what I read as post-traumatic stress, after the threat has disappeared. The realization that the Gestapo would have brutally removed her had she stayed in Paris and the knowledge that they had searched her apartment evoke a heightened emotional response from Stein. During war, Stein explains, everyone in Culoz was preoccupied with the daily tasks and domestic concerns necessary for survival to the extent that there was no time or energy to contemplate remote dangers or any business that did not present itself as an immediate problem. This admission of fear and acknowledgment of persecution at the end of *Wars I Have Seen* leaves the reader with the sense that Stein did in fact harbor an inkling of the dangerousness of her situation during the war and may have had a traumatic response to it after all.

Indeed, Stein and Toklas were subjected to the dangers of occupation.[18] Germans invaded their home and took up residence briefly, but the only casualties were stolen items: an umbrella, a new pair of slippers, peaches, and keys to the front and back doors. Along with an encampment of German soldiers, the residents of Culoz suffer through arbitrary curfew changes and bombardments. Minding curfew becomes a survival strategy for Stein. She recounts buying a watch so that she could keep track of the time: "But now that curfew is at six o'clock, and I am sure to be out on the road somewhere and they do shoot you if you are out I thought it best to have a wrist watch." Her watch brings her "immense pride and joy," though previously she has declared watches to be "kind of dull," because it keeps her safe (203–4). On bombardments Stein comments, "You keep on thinking how quickly anybody can get killed, just as quickly just as very quickly, more quickly even than in a book even much more quickly than in any book, those up there flying and bombing and those down below, with houses tumbling, and burning" (22). The fear of injury and death were omnipresent during bombardments, and the damage to civilian property is noted by Stein. For a period of time living with bombardments becomes a way of life for her.[19]

Stein's relationship with war violence is an odd one. Even though she lived in an occupied country, she was strangely removed from the war, and this remove is keenly felt in *Mrs. Reynolds.* In the midst of bombardments and German soldiers Stein and Toklas and their property remain unscathed. They worry about and pity their friends in Paris because Parisians "are having a good deal of difficulty in keeping alive" (186), whereas in the country conditions are much improved. Stein and Toklas can burn peat for fuel, and they have plenty of food, as Stein details regularly. White bread is scarce, but Stein and Toklas eat well; they even manage to eat cake periodically, and they have food to spare. The town economy provides for everyone: the mayor and the Maquis secure food for the townspeople whenever possible. There is also a bartering system in place, and, if one has money, she can still buy what she needs. Clothing and shoes are scarce, but Stein marvels at how everyone seems to be maintaining their wardrobe and leather shoes. For the most part Stein witnesses less violence and fewer hardships than one might expect for someone in her situation. Being a celebrity helped her case because it offered Stein a certain measure of protection. Stein elaborates on her status: "And one of them [the soldiers] told me that they knew about me because they study my poems along with other American poetry in the public schools" (251). She even signs autographs for the soldiers. At one point Stein claims, "I am a writer and so the French people take care of me" (119). Reaffirming her celebrity status enables Stein to both celebrate her literary achievements and offer an explanation for her relative comfort during World War II.

In *Mrs. Reynolds* and *Wars I Have Seen* Stein is invested in positioning herself as a soldier/veteran. In *Wars I Have Seen* she also revels in a celebration of her canonical status. *Brewsie and Willie,* another war work by Stein, reinforces these motifs. A self-reference to her notoriety is found in *Brewsie and Willie:* "Do you know, said Pauline with great solemnity, you know that Stein woman who says things. Yeah we all know, said Willie" (50). This passage is humorous in its unabashed self-promotion, but it is significant in its desire to affiliate Stein's writings with both a female civilian readership (via Pauline) and a male soldier readership (via Willie). In a text about war Stein literally inserts her authority as author to write about the topic: everyone reads her work and refers to her "with great solemnity." *Brewsie and Willie* reinforces the notion that Stein viewed herself as a civilian and a war veteran, as developed by her earlier works. *Brewsie and Willie,* however, focuses mainly on the perspectives of male soldiers, in contrast to *Mrs. Reynolds* and *Wars I Have Seen.* And yet Stein seems to project her own anxieties and responses to war onto the American soldiers with whom she was so anxious to identify.

Brewsie and Willie consists of fictional dialogues between and conversations among American soldiers stationed in France during World War II.

The soldiers engage in trying to make sense of war and other issues by discussing whatever is on their minds. Brewsie assumes the position of philosopher, and Willie is his sometimes unwilling audience. Willie is crass at times; one of his fellow soldiers, Jo, informs him, "You just bellow, Willie." The same soldier concedes grudgingly that Brewsie, on the other hand, is "foggy" but correct in his assessments: "Yes sometimes I guess Brewsie is right" (17). For the most part Brewsie is intellectual and thoughtful and removed from the more mundane concerns that occupy Willie and the rest of the GIs. But Brewsie is not removed from reality, nor is he afraid to direct attention to unpleasant matters. He says things such as, "Well let's think about how everybody perhaps will get killed in the next war." His concerns sometimes include domestic affairs; he specifically validates the presence of women and children amid war suffering: "But oh dear me, there are the wives and children. Yes there are" (12). Thinking out loud, the work of making meaning, sustains Brewsie, perhaps as it may have for Stein: "I am going to begin to talk and I am just going on talking, that's what I am going to do" (19). Incessant talking keeps Brewsie connected to the other soldiers as well as allowing him to construct a narrative that fortifies him and reaffirms that he is still alive in much the same way that Mrs. Reynolds and Stein herself reached out to passersby. Similarly, Stein enumerates writing as one of her coping strategies: "I did get so that I could not think about the war but just about the stories I was making" ("Winner" 620).

The occasional insertion of a household concern within the soldiers' dialogue serves as an acknowledgment or reminder that the domestic economy is affected by war as well. Donald Paul, a GI, tells a story about a girl who asks him how she can find food to replace potatoes. He replies that she cannot, implying that she must go without (19). While *Brewsie and Willie* focuses on the ideas and issues that Stein ascribes to the province of soldiers' experience, civilian concerns do occasionally rupture the text. In the most developed example Brewsie delineates the differences between a solider and a civilian: "Well anyway, said Brewsie, I often think we soldiers complain, and we complain about what the officers have but we dont complain how we have everything civilians dont have. Civilians, oh hell, what you mean Brewsie. Well dont we have food and clothes and shoes and free parties all the time, they take us everywhere, and eats, and treats, and free everything, subways and theatres and everything and my gracious, my good gracious and no worries" (26–27). The soldiers in *Brewsie and Willie* do worry about bills, available work, and environmental sustainability when thinking about life after the war, but Brewsie downplays the hardships encountered by soldiers when he claims that they have (or should have) no worries. He undercuts soldiers' deprivations in order to emphasize the problems facing civilians. Stein's bias clearly resonates in this passage. As a civilian, she worried over food supply and the cost of everything, and she was limited in terms of luxuries, entertainment, and travel options. Stein is careful to etch out textual space for civilians in her soldiers' dialogue, and in this way she reasserts her focus on and acknowledgment of civilian life in a work that is principally not about civilians or women.

Throughout her war writings—namely, *Lifting Belly, Wars I Have Seen,* and *Mrs. Reynolds*—we see Stein engaging with the sexual politics of war, exposing problematic correlations, and deconstructing false binary relationships concerning male and female identity in light of war. During war it is enough to survive, and nothing actually happens in *Mrs. Reynolds* in terms of plot—except that Mrs. Reynolds endures. And Stein celebrates Mrs. Reynolds's enduring presence in her war novel. She writes Thornton Wilder in 1940, "Mrs. Reynolds is . . . a heroine even if it [the novel] is all about Hitler and Stalin" (qtd. in Whittier-Ferguson, "Stein in Time" n. 39). As Stein's last novel, *Mrs. Reynolds* incorporates and returns to issues Stein raises in former works but in a different configuration that results in different effects: *Mrs. Reynolds* is an emotional response to war without being overtly emotional. Understatement is crucial to the agenda of *Mrs. Reynolds.* No grand accounts of war are given. Historical events must be inferred from the veiled clues in the text. Stein is less concerned with historical accuracy and a relation of events on the macrocosmic level than she is with the domestic, psychological realities from a microcosmic perspective. In *Mrs. Reynolds* Stein fictionalizes war experience to privilege a female response to war: she features *Mrs. Reynolds* as the embodiment of a survivor, and thus Mrs. Reynolds is the heroine of her own war story.

Each of the writers in this study employ different strategies to represent women and their bodies in war and war narrative, but Stein's *Mrs. Reynolds* occupies the position of being the work that speaks to the author's experience of war in the most experiential and embodied manner. *Wars I Have Seen* corroborates and amplifies the very issues that *Mrs. Reynolds* raises. Stein's body is a text that informs Mrs. Reynolds's corporeal experiences (e.g., the effects of food shortages, the acts of scavenging for food and news, and the dangers of traveling) and psychological outlook (e.g., anxiety, latent fear, fatigue, and optimism). But it is in *Mrs. Reynolds* that we find the lengthiest and most developed fictional treatment of a female civilian's life and embodied state, acknowledging Stein's own body, on the home front.

Djuna Barnes could not impart war experience directly to her female characters, nor could she implicate female bodies in traumatic situations, except in circuitous fashion. H.D.'s *Bid Me to Live* and *Trilogy* witness the horrors of war, but H.D. backgrounds World War I in *Bid Me to Live* as the novel progresses, just as *Trilogy* eventually backgrounds World War II and trauma in the second and third long poems to focus on the creation of a female template for feminist writing and healing. *Mrs. Reynolds*, however, obsessively treats World War II; the novel attempts to capture a female perspective of it from the first page to the last. In *Mrs. Reynolds* we have Stein's most experimental fictional work on war and gender, and we encounter the most sustained example in this study of a female response to war. In their works featuring women, war, and trauma, the selected authors offer representations that resonate with important issues concerning identity politics, political investigations into what it means to be a woman writing about, experiencing, and critiquing war. By acknowledging female war trauma and critiquing existing structures that beget war and phallogocentric politics, Barnes, H.D., and Stein create a space for female war writing that insists on female presence.

Afterword

Initially, I became interested in the subject of trauma because of the lack of scholarly attention to it in American women's modernist literature. I found that trauma was discussed in literature in amorphous terms and without a critical framework. Part of the challenge in writing about representations of literary trauma critically is the interdisciplinary focus of contemporary trauma studies. For instance, there is not a codified framework for approaching trauma in literary studies, just as there is not yet a formalized school of trauma studies or set of systematic points or canonical parameters to orient one when thinking about the politics of trauma. My solution to this problem was the reworking and blending together of disparate theories.

There are, however, theorists who discuss trauma in terms of historiography (e.g., Dominick LaCapra), psychoanalysis (e.g., Cathy Caruth), and rhetoric (e.g., Elaine Scarry). The implications of the studies by these theorists can be applied to projects across disciplines. Reflections on historiography enable one to probe the relationship between lived experience and its manifestations in recorded text. But I ultimately discovered that the scope of historiography was limiting for my study of poetry and fiction; for the most part I was not concentrating on biographical sketches or memoirs but on imaginative works. LaCapra, however, is the primary trauma studies theorist I referenced. I favor his nuanced discussion of the problems confronting the trauma studies researcher in *Writing History, Writing Trauma* because his poststructuralist work on trauma coincides with the framework of my project. As a result, I used LaCapra's work to form my definitions of trauma ("founding trauma") and "identity politics," and I tried to keep in mind his important exhortation that a poststructuralist can and *should* make distinctions (distinctions do not necessarily reinforce binary oppositions) instead of insisting on relativism or reductive thinking when discussing traumatic responses. During revisions of this project I omitted Caruth's work. The incorporation of her psychoanalytic, Freudian perspective would have sent this project in a different direction. Instead, I chose to supplement LaCapra's poststructuralist trauma studies approach with Judith Butler's feminist, poststructuralist treatment of bodies in *Bodies That Matter: On the Discursive Limits of "Sex."* Butler's concepts influenced my thinking from the very beginning of this project, and so her work was indispensable to me.

The current project also draws upon Scarry's *The Body in Pain: The Making and Unmaking of the World;* my understanding of war rhetoric and the political and material consequences of war for human bodies is derived solely from Scarry. The literature I discuss in the preceding chapters demonstrates her notions that war rhetoric "unmakes" soldiers just as war injuries "unmake" combatant and noncombatant bodies by emptying them of civilization. The soldier is transformed into a killer, perverting his socialized impulses to abide by law and act peacefully, and the injured person, especially if killed, is unable to gesture to or enact civilizing behaviors because the body has been damaged. This project is indebted to concepts from trauma studies scholars of different academic backgrounds, and the literature I focus on herein demonstrates both the applicability and usefulness of an interdisciplinary trauma studies approach to literature.

Because I am interested in using concepts from a number of theorists who ordinarily are not put into conversation with one another in a single study, refining the theoretical framework was perhaps the most challenging aspect of this project. I discovered that what it really needed—and what I really wanted to say—was that poststructuralism could exist in a kind of hybridized and harmonious relationship with embodiment theories, provided that the terms are carefully defined and the ways in which the theories intersect are clarified as needed. Elizabeth Grosz argues for a synthesis of the interior (consciousness) and the exterior (corporeality), and she sees embodiment as incorporating this synthesis in conjunction with lived experience. Thus, I built upon and refined Grosz's understanding of embodiment when I introduced and combined LaCapra's notions of trauma, Butler's notions of gender and performance, and Scarry's notions of war as a discursively covert business of injury that results in the unmaking of civilization. The definitions I have formulated from the work of these theorists can be found in the introduction.

Another discovery I made early on, while researching the individual authors and texts, was the extent to which women in war, especially women's responses to and representations of war and trauma, had been neglected. Works such as H.D.'s *Bid Me to Live* and Stein's *Mrs. Reynolds*, for instance, are currently out of print, and the published scholarship on most of the selected works in this project is thus far either sparse or limited in the discussions of war and trauma. The study began to take the shape of a recovery project, with the revisionist aspect (women creating space in patriarchal war narrative and reconfiguring it) following as the project developed. From the beginning I had also planned to write about depictions of women's bodies. After working as a grant writer in the administrative office of a domestic violence shelter, I developed an awareness of the cultural inscriptions that plague female bodies and the often culturally unintelligible responses by victims to sexual or physical trauma. I finally settled on the world wars as the impetus for female responses to trauma-producing events that would take into account female bodies. Because I was interested in approaching my project from a feminist perspective, I viewed war as a fitting subject in that it was a masculinist project that my selected female authors engaged with and revised in their own poetry and prose to varying degrees and for slightly different purposes. The project evolved and changed from my initial conception of it; it became more about how the writers *represented* the gender politics of war and trauma than an examination of how the selected authors suffered and witnessed, although witnessing is an important act for H.D. and Stein and perhaps for Barnes too.

As a side note, I would like to add that by no means do I wish to argue that preference should be given to these female civilian authors over male combatant writers. I certainly do not wish to reverse any binary relationships, nor do I want to claim that civilians suffer more than soldiers in combat. What I would like to see is an opening up of what I have generically called "war literature" and "patriarchal war narrative" to include both artistic responses to war by women and witness accounts from the home front by women, some of whom did suffer from trauma.

Barnes maintains she suffered, but she avoided World War I and most of World War II. Thus, the focus of my study changed to include a poststructuralist analysis of not only trauma and female bodies but also the ways in which war itself was construed in the text. I saw a genealogy emerge that connected Barnes, H.D., and Stein to each other in a larger project of revisionist responses to war and gender. I conclude this project with the understanding that the selected women writers protested war (war as destructive and perverse, war as traumatic, and war as quotidian) in different treatments (surrealist, epic, and confessional prose and poetry) and that these treatments invariably touched upon aspects of female embodiment.

The various depictions of bodies bespeak the political engagement of the female characters with war. The bodies become personally political in the poems and novels featured because they directly (in the works of H.D. and Stein) or indirectly (in the works of Barnes) comment upon war in the domestic economy. The bodies are marked by war ravages: bodily injury, psychological and emotional distress, and intermittent fear. Barnes's Robin Vote resorts to dissolute behavior, devolving into an animal state at the end of *Nightwood*. H.D. touches upon the fear of injury and psychological distress during war in *Trilogy* before moving on to consider antidotes to trauma. Lastly, in *Mrs. Reynolds* Stein catalogues the daily rituals and experiences of living on the home front during war, periodically giving us glimpses of—and sometimes admitting to—the fear that French civilians learned to live with during World War II.

The significance of this project lies in its construction of a genealogy of modernist American women writers and their treatments of war. Never before have Barnes, H.D., and Stein been considered together in a study of war or trauma. Barnes begins the work of deconstructing gendered binary constructions and inserting women into war narrative, and H.D. and Stein continue this trajectory by cultivating more pronounced depictions of women and their bodies in war narrative. The development of actualized female characters progresses steadily from Barnes to Stein; Barnes imagines war, and Stein witnesses it, but all of the authors in this study treat war, trauma, and female embodiment in their literary output. The literature these writers produce foregrounds the identity politics inherent in war narratives and representations of women and trauma in wartime. The ramifications of this study are an increased awareness of who was writing about war, if we expand the definition of what constitutes war writing, and the shape that responses to war took in avant-garde literature of the early twentieth century. Women writers and their writing on war should be consistently included in war anthologies and otherwise showcased because female civilian perspectives provide alternative viewpoints on an often neglected aspect of war: life on the home front in wartime.

The experimental women writers in this study produced artistic and moving representations that protest war, contest female absence in war narrative, and advocate acknowledgment of female war-related trauma. As such, the works of the selected authors are fraught with political implications, especially in regard to marginalized identity. In short war writing by American women writers of the early twentieth century provides a bigger picture of how war was thought about, experienced, and construed. As a result, their works are relevant to modernist studies, American studies, women's studies, and perhaps to our own political climate of the twenty-first century.

Broadly speaking, this project brings together in new ways sometimes undervalued works by female modernist authors. I am not interested in new historicism so much as I am in a feminist trauma studies perspective that incorporates embodiment theory and locates itself within a broad poststructuralist framework. This project fuses two apparently different ideologies or modes of inquiry (poststructuralism and embodiment theories) to inquire into the nature of responses to war and trauma. I integrated these two theoretical schools because I did not want to deny the real-world materiality of the (sometimes suffering) female body during wartime, but I did want to examine critically how female embodiment is construed in the selected poems and novels. Perhaps this study will interest scholars of English and women's studies because it takes seriously the social constructionist logic that texts shape how we think about ourselves and the world, and it provides analyses of women's literature through feminist theoretical lenses.

My discussions of the primary texts in this study form a significant contribution. The most common way to study *Trilogy* is as a feminist work—but much can be made of the poststructuralist play and poetics of the text and the insistence on performing female bodies and identities as a response and antidote to the traumatic experiences of war and patriarchal narrative. I add to the feminist discussion of *Trilogy* by discussing the poststructuralist play of female bodies and identities as well as exploring H.D.'s emotional and literary responses to trauma. As for Stein's *Mrs. Reynolds*, very little has been written about it, and my study contributes a discussion of another neglected work to not only Stein studies but to American modernist women's literature. Of all the works selected for this project, Barnes's *Nightwood* is the most celebrated. Over a hundred articles treat *Nightwood*, but no one has yet ventured the argument I make here. Many critics comment on the grotesque aspects of the novel and its bizarre characters, but I have argued that the grotesque and the bizarre are part of a response to trauma, a reflection of a grotesque and bizarre surrealist world, duly manifesting in the psychological states of the characters and subtly attributed to the ramifications of war.

Modernism is an era of manifestos and narratives, and these women writers very much believed in narratives—narratives that reconfigure identities. Indeed, Barnes, H.D., and Stein are pivotal in their contributions to identity discursive formations. They write women into their texts and thus create space for a reworking of identities in poetry and prose. These authors contribute to identity discursive formations because they claim authority for women to write about and discuss war as well as challenging gender roles and validating women's responses to trauma. Barnes, H.D., and Stein embraced a revisionist project that critiques patriarchal structures and rewrites patriarchal narrative to include stories by women about women and their relationships to war. The selected women writers engage in identity politics, and in their literary output they imagined and created new representations of women in modernist American literature.

— *Notes* —

INTRODUCTION

1. Elizabeth Grosz in *Volatile Bodies* concurs, "I would contend that without some acknowledgment of the formative role of experience in the establishment of knowledges, feminism has no grounds from which to dispute patriarchal norms" (94). The act of drawing upon personal experience and personal observations validates otherwise foreclosed or unacknowledged identities and experiences while enhancing knowledge and enlarging understanding of different identities and different kinds of experiences. Grosz refrains from "bracketing off" experience and setting it aside (95). In this way personal experience becomes political.

2. Stein's *Mrs. Reynolds* is certainly in need of critical attention. Barnes's *Nightwood* is not typically written about as a war novel, although I am not the only one to assert that it does, indeed, treat World War I trauma and World War II anxiety. H.D.'s *Trilogy* is receiving increasing attention and is probably the most read and taught work under examination here.

3. There are exceptions within the last ten years, although the number of anthologies that do not include war writing by women is staggering. Please see the following for in-print anthologies that include a selection of primary work by American women war writers: Lorrie Goldensohn's *American War Poetry: An Anthology* (Columbia UP, 2006); George Clarke's *A Treasury of War Poetry: British and American Poems of the World War, 1914–1919* (Kessinger, 2005); James Meredith's *Understanding the Literature of World War II: A Student Casebook to Issues, Sources, and Historical Documents* (Greenwood, 1999); Clare Tylee's *War Plays by Women: An International Anthology* (Routledge, 1999); Jon Silkin's revised *The Penguin Book of First World War Poetry* (Penguin, 1997); and Trudi Tate's *Women, Men, and the Great War: An Anthology of Short Stories* (Manchester UP, 1996).

CHAPTER 1: CIRCUMVENTING THE CIRCUMSCRIPTION OF MARGINALIZATION

1. I take my definitions of the adjective *perverse* from the *Oxford English Dictionary.* Specifically, I am referencing the following definitions: in regard to a deviant identity or deviant behavior, 1. a. "Of a person, action, etc.: going or disposed to go against what is reasonable, logical, expected, or required; contrary, fickle, irrational"; and in regard to a corrupted society (and to war later in the chapter), 2. a. "Contrary to what is morally right or good; wicked, evil, debased."

2. This scene is found in the "Drafts" section of *Nightwood: The Original Version and Related Drafts.* I use the drafts as an extension of the original text because the publication of the facsimile edition includes the related drafts as parts of the original text. Any citation for *Nightwood* after p. 139 comes from the supplemental material found in the facsimile edition.

3. The major exceptions are discussions by Margaret Bockting, Erin Carlston, and Jane Marcus. Bockting positions *Nightwood* as a war novel, with Barnes as a female author examining binary constructions in war in connection to O'Connor as soldier. Carlston traces the trope of fascism through the novel, arguing that *Nightwood* "mimics many of fascism's favorite tropes"—two of which, decadence and decline, can be discerned in the style of the novel (43). Marcus discusses identities of alterity and correlates these othered identities to the political climate that would engender World War II.

4. See the facsimile edition of *Nightwood* for these scenes.

5. Barnes considered "Bow Down" as a title for what became *Nightwood*. Instead, the first chapter was given that title. Such a title resonates with fascist ideology, subservience, and extermination. This interpretation is especially significant in that chap. 1 details Felix's "disqualification" and his need to bow "low enough" so "the great past might mend a little" (Barnes 9).

6. See pp. 130–36 in the chapter "Go Down, Matthew" for the bar scene in which a drunk, angry, and hysteric O'Connor confronts the public with its persecution of difference and its bloodshed. He predicts "the end—mark my words—now *nothing, but wrath and weeping!*" (136).

7. Responding to Felix's preoccupation with immortality, convention, and habit, O'Connor responds, "We heap reproaches on the person who breaks it [habit], saying that in so doing he has broken the image—of our safety" (94).

8. Ironically, Barnes once felt no shame about harboring a lesbian (or heterosexual) identity. According to Antonia White, "Djuna told me she had no feeling of guilt whatever about sex, about going to bed with any man or woman she wanted, but that she felt extremely guilty and ashamed of drinking" (qtd. in Herring 239).

9. Since 1983 Barnes critics have agreed for the most part that Robin's counterpart is Wood and Jenny's counterpart is Eleanor Fitzgerald, nicknamed Fitzie. For her part Barnes told O'Neal more than sixty years after the publication of *Nightwood* that Robin is Wood, Nora is modeled after Henriette Metcalf, and O'Connor's counterpart is Dan Mahoney (28).

10. I follow the practice of William Carlos Williams, personally acquainted with Elsa von Freytag-Loringhoven, in referring to her as "the Baroness," as she was also known by her contemporaries. See chap. 28 in *The Autobiography of William Carlos Williams.*

Although she published poetry in *The Little Review* and *transition*, von Freytag-Loringhoven is known primarily as a dadaist, especially in her roles as collaborator and friend of Marcel Duchamp. Barnes's affair with Wood lasted from 1922 to 1928, and her friendship with the Baroness spanned the years 1923 through 1927 (Gammel 356). Von Freytag-Loringhoven and Barnes developed a close friendship, with Barnes ultimately becoming the Baroness's literary executor at the Baroness's request.

11. For an additional and recent discussion by a von Freytag–Loringhoven scholar on the influence of the Baroness on the character of Robin, see Irene Gammel, *Baroness Elsa: Gender, Dada, and Everyday Modernity—A Cultural Biography* (Cambridge, MA: MIT P, 2003), 357–59. For a discussion by the Baroness herself on her life, see Elsa von Freytag-Loringhoven, *Baron-*

ess Elsa, ed. Paul I. Hjartarson and Douglas O. Spettigue (Ottawa, Canada: Oberon P, 1992). The editors of *Baroness Elsa* acknowledge their debt to DeVore's 1982 article on *Nightwood;* it piqued their interest in examining the Baroness's papers, which are housed, along with Barnes's papers, at the University of Maryland at College Park. Critics of *Nightwood* tend to read Wood as a primary source for Robin because Barnes acknowledged that she was a model; see n. 9.

12. Additional comparisons abound. The Baroness and Robin are described in similar physical terms; each possesses the figure of a boy, startling blue eyes, beastly terror, and the title of "Baronin" (DeVore 80–81). Robin also wears costumes that the Baroness would have worn (Gammel 357): "Her clothes were of a period that he could not quite place. She wore feathers of the kind his mother had worn, flattened sharply to her face" with skirts made of "heaving silks that made her seem newly ancient" (Barnes, *Nightwood* 40). The Baroness's body odor corresponds to Robin's body "perfume" that "was of the quality of that earth-flesh, fungi, which smells of captured dampness and yet is so dry, overcast with the odour of oil of amber," and constitutes "the infected carrier of the past: before her the structure of our head and jaws ache—we feel that we could eat her, she who is eaten death returning" (34, 36). The parallels between the Baroness and Robin are instructive; we can potentially read the traumatized Baroness onto the character of Robin. Like her, Robin is construed as a traumatized "somnambule," emotionally and psychologically damaged during the war years.

13. As a possible final nod to the Baroness, the last chapter is steeped in dada, "charged with dada outrage and opaqueness." Robin is even attributed with the Baroness's barking laughter. According to Gammel, "Recognizing herself in Robin Vote, Wood was so shocked by the proximity with the grotesque Baroness that she slapped Barnes's face after reading the novel" (358).

CHAPTER 2: VALIDATING FEMALE WAR EXPERIENCE THROUGH LITERARY WITNESSING

1. Following the trend in H.D. scholarship, I will give page numbers instead of line numbers for *Trilogy* references.

2. According to Adalaide Morris, "First called *War Trilogy* and then, more simply, *Trilogy*, this poem can be interpreted as something like the signal the building superintendent expected to find: a warning, a command, an incitement to concerted action" ("Signaling" 121). She suggests that *Trilogy* may be read as working "to surface the terrors and redirect them to constructive ends" (*How to Live* 111). I also read H.D. as advocate, but I read *Trilogy* as an enactment of her agenda. I argue that H.D. creates a literary template for the reclamation of women's voices and bodies, eliciting embodied responses to trauma, within war narrative. Norman Holmes Pearson considered *Trilogy* a significant contribution to "civilian war literature" (qtd. in Hollenberg 22).

3. DuPlessis reads H.D. as engaged in "rebalancing the religious and prophetic tradition between the genders" in "The Flowering of the Rod" (89). I interpret this rebalancing act as

a result of H.D.'s insertion of women into war narrative in *Trilogy* at large. Her vision of war as a problem that has traditionally dismissed female suffering and participation, coupled with her vision of the female poet as prophetic, leads her to cast the female poet-prophet as a healing visionary who investigates and creates a healing narrative in response to the war trauma suffered by women. Ultimately, the poet-prophet rewrites religious narrative to accommodate women in a search for wholeness and empowerment.

4. The reader is invited in the first-person-plural identification: "By using the inclusive pronoun 'we' without a continuous and always specific referent, the poem invites the reader to read him-/herself into the pronoun, and thus establish his/her space within the text" (Hardin 156). Creating a space for women (and men) in the text correlates with the desire to create a text devoid of circumscribing sexual politics. On the other hand, I maintain that H.D. refers mainly to a collective of female artists because it is women who have traditionally been circumscribed, marginalized, and excluded from the poetic body politic, especially in relation to war poetry or war narratives. I concur with Marina Sbisà's conclusions in her linguistic study of *Trilogy* that H.D. "has pursued and practised" feminine subjectivity, often her own, throughout the work (112). According to Sbisà, "Throughout *Trilogy*, we often find first-person pronouns or possessives. In many cases, the enunciating subject thus signaled is aligned with the authorial subject and acts as a facet of the author's own enunciating subjectivity" (94).

CHAPTER 3: A WAR HEROINE IN THE DOMESTIC ECONOMY

1. I will follow the practice of other scholars of *Lifting Belly* and list page numbers instead of line numbers for this unnumbered poem.

2. Nicola Rehling remarks upon the futility of attempting to decode Stein's work: "Stein's writing resists comprehensive deciphering because she deliberately frustrates readerly expectations and in so doing prevents her texts from being appropriated into a singular meaning. In fact, the final line of *Lifting Belly* reads 'In the midst of writing there is merriment,' so that Stein may seduce the reader into believing s/he has construed the 'code' in *Lifting Belly* but then dislodges any assertion of power over the text and playfully informs the reader that her poem will remain elusive" (81).

3. The persona and her partner are identifiable as women through various clues in the text—for example: "Will you exchange purses. You know I like to please you" (57).

4. John Whittier-Ferguson in "Stein in Time" and Richard Bridgman in *Gertrude Stein in Pieces* both date the composition of *Mrs. Reynolds* during these years, although the *Yale Gertrude Stein* gives 1940–42 as the date of composition. See Whittier-Ferguson's article "Stein in Time" (n. 1). Bridgman explains: "The Yale editors have dated *Mrs. Reynolds* 1940–42, but the eleventh section refers to 23 December 1942, and the twelfth and thirteenth sections were almost certainly written more than a year later. For these concluding sections have references in them springing up of the Resistance, the German debacle in Russia, rumors of the Nazis weakening, and the comforting hum of bombers on their way to Italy" (324).

Random House held off on publishing *Mrs. Reynolds* because it recalled the avant-garde experimental writing of the *Tender Buttons* period, "when Stein's writing was too experimental to sell" (Davis 571). On May 3, 1943, *Time* magazine announced that the typescript for *Mrs. Reynolds* had been smuggled out of occupied France and given to the publisher Bennett Cerf via Sweden; Cerf "could make nothing of it," however, and "felt it 'could probably be read from either end'" (Burns, Dydo, and Rice 404). He wanted to publish it anyway but was prevented from doing so because of the wartime paper shortage.

There was speculation in the unsigned parody (mimicking the bootlegged copy of *Mrs. Reynolds*) "Talk of the Town" in the February 19, 1944, edition of the *New Yorker* that the novel was not commercial enough to warrant publication during a paper shortage: "The name of the novel is Mrs. Reynolds [*sic*] but it would do you no good to go into Bertrano's and ask for Mrs. Reynolds until after the war. While the war is going on Random House wants to print Quentin Reynolds, alas. Bennett B. Toklas the editor of Random House may not know much but he knows that much. He knows that Quentin Reynolds will sell better than Mrs. Reynolds not Mrs. Quentin Reynolds but Gertrude's Mrs. Reynolds" (qtd. in Burns, Dydo, and Rice 404). *Mrs. Reynolds* first appeared in 1952 as part of the Yale University Press collection of Stein's unpublished work.

5. As other critics have pointed out, Stein does not examine race, class, or sexuality in this work in any satisfying way. My thesis differs markedly from the excellent work of Davis, Diedrich, Olson, and Whittier-Ferguson on *Mrs. Reynolds* and Stein's other war writings because of my emphasis on *Mrs. Reynolds* as a work principally concerned with a narrative of survival, responding to trauma (when it surfaces) through experiments in formal conventions and language conventions to give a poststructuralist and embodied account of noncombatant life from a woman's perspective. I agree with Diedrich, who does not argue from a poststructuralist perspective or even about *Mrs. Reynolds*, when she claims that Stein "shattered the belief that an event like World War II can still be reconstructed according to the rules of . . . logocentrism, that is, the cultural hegemony of sense—rationality, linearity, and hierarchical order" (92). I believe this assessment of *Wars I Have Seen* is more apt with regard to *Mrs. Reynolds*. Stein defies the binary oppositions of man and war versus woman and home.

6. Angel Harper is a stand-in for Adolf Hitler in the same way that Joseph Lane resembles Joseph Stalin.

7. See Stein's "Introduction to the Speeches of Maréchal Pétain," *Modernism/modernity* 3.3 (1994): 94. Stein never finished her proposed translations of Pétain's speeches.

8. Davis notes that "the majority of Stein's readers, publishers, and critics agreed that her aesthetic concerns in a text such as *Mrs. Reynolds* precluded her engagement with historical or political events in any serious way" (571). Critics who claim that Stein's last novel is devoid of historicity base their argument on the experimental aspects of the novel and its lack of specificity and putative referentiality. They read the formal experiments as anti-referential, usurping any focus on a historical account or historical representation. Like Davis, I argue that *Mrs. Reynolds* is very much rooted in history. Davis asserts that Stein "engaged in the politics of the period precisely by bringing her aesthetic concerns to her discussion of war"

(570). War thus informs every artistic decision Stein made in *Mrs. Reynolds,* from content to stylistic concerns. *Mrs. Reynolds* pivots on the experience of war and the effects of war in all its manifestations in noncombatant life.

9. See p. 95 of Diedrich's article and p. 165 in *Mrs. Reynolds.*

10. A portion of the telling passage follows: "it was an enormous moon and a cold moon although spring had come, and the moon was called a red moon and a rough moon a Russian moon and Angel Harper knew that when he had been fourteen he had first seen this moon to know it as such a moon and now Angel Harper was fifty-two and spring was come and it was true, the big moon the enormous moon the cold moon the red moon the Russian moon was a moon, Angel Harper hoped it might be noon, but was it noon, no said Angel Harper and he hoped it was yesterday but no it was not yesterday it was today, and Angel Harper could not go away" (Stein, *Mrs. Reynolds* 259–60). Copeland recognizes historical French sentiments in *Mrs. Reynolds.* From 1940 to 1942 Stalin would have been linked to Hitler in the minds of the French through the 1940 alliance between Russia and Germany. After Hitler invaded Russia, "the shadow of the second man, Stalin, became less ominous to the French" (Copeland 163).

11. Whittier-Ferguson notes that Stein was a friend of the painter Francis Rose, who, in turn, was friends with Ernst Roehm, leader of Hitler's storm troopers. Stein had also befriended Bernard Faÿ, wartime director of the Bibliothèque Nationale and an acquaintance of Marshal Philippe Pétain. According to Whittier-Ferguson, "There is every reason to believe that the influence of both men, particularly that of Faÿ, helped preserve Stein's and Toklas's property and physical safety throughout the war" ("Stein in Time" 120).

12. Mrs. Reynolds exhibits patriotic notions about George Washington: "She had when she was a little girl thought it would be wonderful it would have been wonderful to live in the time of George Washington." She describes him as "first in peace first in war and first in the hearts of his countrymen" (59). He is invoked because of the war setting of the novel. Mr. Reynolds, too, prefers to tell three stories treating the United States: one discussing the production of American goods, the second dealing with the Civil War, and the last story narrating an American imperial impulse related to trade (58).

13. See pp. 160–62 for what the prophecy of Saint Odile foretells.

14. See Davis's article, n. 19, as evidence of Stein's interest in prophecies.

15. See pp. 196, 211, and 233.

16. Elizabeth Gregory offers another interpretation of Stein's language use. As Gregory observes: "Stein's language has also been linked to the Kristevan semiotic and understood to re-create through its rhythms and its play with sound the pleasures of vocal interaction within a mother-child dyad. Such an honouring of the pre-symbolic over mature language use has also been read as a challenge to standard hierarchies" (263). Such an interpretation would privilege the feminine component of the response to war rather than a trauma-induced component. While I am persuaded that Stein writes in ways that challenge standard hierarchies, I am unconvinced that a Kristevan approach opens up productive readings of *Mrs. Reynolds.*

17. Stein describes Mrs. Reynolds's obsession with food: "Mrs. Reynolds said that thinking about food, what is food where is food and food as food made one nervous. It said Mrs. Reynolds makes me sad that when I am condoling with some one whom I have not seen for such a long time and now she is all alone I think of whether I can buy some food from her. Food said Mrs. Reynolds food makes you think of food and thinking of food makes you ask for food and asking for food makes you nervous and being nervous makes you feel as if you were a beggar and feeling that you are a beggar makes you know what begging is, and begging makes you know you are rich enough to pay, and anyway said Mrs. Reynolds food makes you nervous, yes it does" (308).

18. See p. 196 for Stein's brief encounter with a German deserter in her home, and see pp. 211–12 for Stein's description of German soldiers quartered in her home. Also see pp. 215–16 for an account of German soldiers swarming over Stein's property. To illustrate the dangerousness of the situation, Stein details her dog's reactions. Her dog, Basket, "was so horrified that he could not even bark," and "he just sat and shivered." Stein frets that "perhaps Basket will never bark again" after his traumatic encounter with the German soldiers (216). In a sense Basket becomes a victim, and his victimization is the closest Stein comes to voicing a sense of dread and fear during occupation in *Wars I Have Seen.*

19. See p. 170 for Stein's disinterest in news of bombings (because it is part of her everyday reality); see p. 192 for the selling of Stein's car (she sells it to a Red Cross worker who desperately needs a vehicle to continue his work when his own car is smashed in a bombardment); see p. 205 for Stein's mention of "explosions all around us"; see p. 227 for the devastation caused and fear generated by bombardments; and see p. 189 for Stein's familiarity with bomb shelters.

— *Bibliography* —

Abraham, Julie. "'We are Americans': Gertrude, *Brewsie and Willie.*" *Modern Fiction Studies* 42.3 (1996): 508–27.

———. "'Woman, Remember You': Djuna Barnes and History." *Silence and Power: A Reevaluation of Djuna Barnes.* Ed. Mary Lynn Broe. Carbondale: Southern Illinois P, 1991. 252–68.

Acheson, Susan. "'Conceived at the Grave's Edge': The Esoteric Eschatology of H.D.'s *Trilogy.*" *Literature and Theology* 12.2 (1998): 187–204.

Altman, Meryl. "A Book of Repulsive Jews? Rereading *Nightwood.*" *Review of Contemporary Fiction* 13.3 (1993): 160–71.

Balaev, Michelle. "Trends in Literary Trauma Theory." *Mosaic: A Journal for the Comparative Study of Literature* 41.2 (2008): 149–67.

Barnes, Djuna. "Matron's Primer." Rev. of *Wars I Have Seen,* by Gertrude Stein. *Contemporary Jewish Record* (June 1945). Rpt. in *The Critical Response to Gertrude Stein.* Ed. Kirk Curnutt. Westport, CT: Greenwood, 2000. 136–38.

———. *Nightwood: The Original Version and Related Drafts.* Ed. Cheryl J. Plumb. Normal, IL: Dalkey Archive, 1995.

———. "War in Paris (1939)." *Collected Poems with Notes toward the Memoirs.* Ed. Phillip Herring and Osías Stutman. Madison: U of Wisconsin P, 2005. 263–70.

Barnstone, Aliki. "A Note on H.D.'s Life." *Trilogy.* By H.D. New York: New Directions, 1998. 202–6.

———. "Reader's Notes." *Trilogy,* by H.D. New York: New Directions, 1998. 173–201.

Benstock, Shari. *Women of the Left Bank: Paris, 1900–1940.* Austin: U of Texas P, 1986.

Blyn, Robin. "*Nightwood*'s Freak Dandies: Decadence in the 1930s." *Modernism/modernity* 15.3 (2008): 503–26.

Bochner, Jay, and Justin D. Edwards, eds. *American Modernism across the Arts.* New York: Peter Lang, 1999.

Bockting, Margaret. "The Great War and Modern Gender Consciousness: The Subversive Tactics of Djuna Barnes." *Mosaic: A Journal for the Comparative Study of Literature* 30.3 (1997): 21–38.

Boehnen, Scott. "'H.D., War Poet' and the 'Language Fantasy' of *Trilogy.*" *Sagetrieb* 14.1–2 (1995): 179–200.

Bonney, Therese. "Gertrude Stein in France." 1942. *Gertrude Stein Remembered.* Ed. Lisa Simon. Lincoln: U of Nebraska P, 1994. 176–80.

Bridgman, Richard. *Gertrude Stein in Pieces.* New York: Oxford UP, 1970.

Brown, Dennis. "HD's *Trilogy:* Modern Gnosticism?" *Literature and Theology* 10.4 (1996): 351–60.

Buck, Claire. *H.D. and Freud: Bisexuality and a Feminine Discourse.* New York: St. Martin's, 1991.

Bürger, Peter. *Theory of the Avant-Garde.* Trans. Michael Shaw. Theory and History of Literature. Minneapolis: U of Minnesota P, 1984.

Burns, Edward, ed. *The Letters of Gertrude Stein and Carl Van Vechten, 1913–1946.* Vol. 2. New York: Columbia UP, 1986.

Burns, Edward, Ulla E. Dydo, and William Rice, eds. *The Letters of Gertrude Stein and Thornton Wilder.* New Haven: Yale UP, 1996.

Butler, Judith. *Bodies That Matter: On the Discursive Limits of "Sex."* New York: Routledge, 1993.

———. "Performative Acts and Gender Constitution: An Essay in Phenomenology and Feminist Theory." *Writing on the Body: Female Embodiment and Feminist Theory.* Ed. Katie Conboy, Nadia Medina, and Sarah Stanbury. New York: Columbia UP, 1997. 401–17.

Carlston, Erin G. *Thinking Fascism: Sapphic Modernism and Fascist Modernity.* Stanford: Stanford UP, 1998.

Caruth, Cathy, ed. *Trauma: Explorations in Memory.* Baltimore: Johns Hopkins UP, 1995.

———. *Unclaimed Experience: Trauma, Narrative, and History.* Baltimore: Johns Hopkins UP, 1996.

Cixous, Hélenè, and Catherine Clément. *The Newly Born Woman.* Trans. Betsy Wing. Theory and History of Literature. Vol. 24. Minneapolis: U of Minnesota P, 1986.

Clark, Suzanne. *Sentimental Modernism: Women Writers and the Revolution of the Word.* Bloomington: Indiana UP, 1991.

Cohn, Carol. "Wars, Wimps, and Women: Talking Gender and Thinking War." *Gendering War Talk.* Ed. Miriam Cooke and Angela Woollacott. Princeton: Princeton UP, 1993. 227–46.

Copeland, Carolyn Faunce. *Language and Time and Gertrude Stein.* Iowa City: U of Iowa P, 1975.

Cubilié, Anne. *Women Witnessing Terror: Testimony and the Cultural Politics of Human Rights.* New York: Fordham UP, 2005.

Damon, S. Foster. *Amy Lowell: A Chronicle with Extracts from Her Correspondence.* Cambridge: Riverside, 1935.

Davis, Phoebe Stein. "'Even Cake Gets to Have Another Meaning': History, Narrative, and 'Daily Living' in Gertrude Stein's World War II Writings." *Modern Fiction Studies* 44.3 (1998): 568–607.

Dawes, James. *The Language of War: Literature and Culture in the U.S. from the Civil War through World War II.* Cambridge: Harvard UP, 2002.

DeKoven, Marianne. *A Different Language: Gertrude Stein's Experimental Writing.* Madison: U of Wisconsin P, 1983.

———. "Introduction: Transformations of Gertrude Stein." *Modern Fiction Studies* 42 (1996): 469–83.

———. *Rich and Strange: Gender, History, Modernism.* Princeton: Princeton UP, 1991.

De Lauretis, Teresa. "*Nightwood* and the 'Terror' of Uncertain Signs." *Critical Inquiry* 34.5 (2008): 117–29.

Derrida, Jacques. *Of Grammatology.* Trans. Gayatri Spivak. Baltimore: Johns Hopkins UP, 1998.

Detloff, Madelyn. "'Father, Don't You See I'm Burning?' Identification and Remembering in H.D.'s World War II Writing." *Incest and the Literary Imagination.* Ed. Elizabeth Barnes. Gainesville: UP of Florida, 2002. 249–80.

DeVore, Lynn. "The Backgrounds of *Nightwood:* Robin, Felix, and Nora." *Journal of Modern Literature* 10.1 (1983): 71–90.

Dickie, Margaret. *Stein, Bishop, and Rich: Lyrics of Love, War, and Place.* Chapel Hill: U of North Carolina P, 1997.

Diedrich, Maria. "'A Book in Translation about Eggs and Butter': Gertrude Stein's World War II." *Women and War: The Changing Status of American Women from the 1930s to the 1950s.* Ed. Maria Diedrich and Dorothea Fischer-Hornung. New York: Berg, 1990. 87–106.

Dillon, Sarah. "Palimpsesting: Reading and Writing Lives in H.D.'s 'Murex: War and Postwar London (circa 1916–1926).'" *Critical Survey* 19.1 (2007): 29–39.

Di Prete, Laura. *"Foreign Bodies": Trauma, Corporeality, and Textuality in Contemporary American Culture.* Literary Criticism and Cultural Theory. New York: Routledge, 2006.

DuPlessis, Rachel Blau. *H.D.: The Career of That Struggle.* Bloomington: Indiana UP, 1986.

———. *Gender, Races and Religious Cultures in Modern American Poetry, 1908–1934.* Cambridge: Cambridge UP, 2001.

Dydo, Ulla E., with William Rice. *Gertrude Stein: The Language that Rises, 1923–1934.* Evanston, IL: Northwestern UP, 2003.

Engelbrecht, Penelope J. "'Lifting Belly Is a Language': The Postmodern Lesbian Subject." *Feminist Studies* 16.1 (1990): 85–115.

Eysteinsson, Astradur. *The Concept of Modernism.* Ithaca: Cornell UP, 1990.

Felman, Shoshana, and Dori Laub. *Testimony: Crises of Witnessing in Literature: Psychoanalysis, and History.* New York: Routledge, 1992.

Felski, Rita. *The Gender of Modernity.* Cambridge: Harvard UP, 1995.

Field, Andrew. *Djuna: The Life and Times of Djuna Barnes.* New York: Putnam, 1983.

Fleischer, Georgette. "Djuna Barnes and T. S. Eliot: The Politics and Poetics of *Nightwood.*" *Studies in the Novel* 30.3 (1998): 405–37.

Forché, Carolyn. *Against Forgetting: Twentieth-Century Poetry of Witness.* New York: Norton, 1993.

Frankenberg, Lloyd. Foreword. *Mrs. Reynolds and Five Earlier Novelettes.* By Gertrude Stein. New Haven: Yale UP, 1952. v–xii.

Freytag-Loringhoven, Elsa, von. "Selections from Letters, with Foreword by Djuna Barnes." *transition* 11 (1928): 19–30.

Friedman, Susan Stanford. *Penelope's Web: Gender, Modernity, H.D.'s Fiction.* Cambridge: Cambridge UP, 1990.

———. *Psyche Reborn: The Emergence of H.D.* Bloomington: Indiana UP, 1981.

Fussell, Paul. *The Great War and Modern Memory.* New York: Oxford UP, 1975.

Gambrell, Alice. *Women Intellectuals, Modernism, and Difference: Transatlantic Culture, 1919–1945.* Cultural Margins. Cambridge: Cambridge UP, 1997.

Gammel, Irene. *Baroness Elsa: Gender, Dada, and Everyday Modernity—A Cultural Biography.* Cambridge: MIT P, 2002.

Goldman, Dorothy, Jane Gledhill, and Judith Hattaway. *Women Writers and the Great War.* New York: Twayne, 1995.

Golier, Julia A., Rachel Yehuda, and Steven Southwick. "Memory and Posttraumatic Stress Disorder." *Trauma and Memory: Clinical and Legal Controversies.* Ed. Paul S. Appelbaum, Lisa A. Uyehara, and Mark R. Elin. New York: Oxford UP, 1997. 225–42.

Graham, Sarah H. S. "'We have a secret. We are alive': H.D.'s *Trilogy* as a Response to War." *Texas Studies in Literature and Language* 44.2 (2002): 161–210.

Gregory, Elizabeth. "Gertrude Stein and War." *Women's Fiction and the Great War.* Ed. Suzanne Raitt and Trudi Tate. New York: Oxford UP, 1997. 263–81.

Grosz, Elizabeth. *Volatile Bodies: Toward a Corporeal Feminism.* Bloomington: Indiana UP, 1994.

Guest, Barbara. *Herself Defined: The Poet H.D. and Her World.* Garden City, NY: Doubleday, 1984.

Gygax, Franziska. *Gender and Genre in Gertrude Stein.* Contributions in Women's Studies. Westport, CT: Greenwood, 1998.

Hanley, Lynne. *Writing War: Fiction, Gender, and Memory.* Amherst: U of Massachusetts P, 1991.

Hanrahan, Mairéad. "Djuna Barnes' *Nightwood:* The Cruci-Fiction of the Jew." *Paragraph* 24.1 (2001): 32–49.

Hardin, Michael. "H.D.'s *Trilogy:* Speaking through the Margins." *Sagetrieb* 15.1–2 (1996): 151–60.

H[ilda]. D[oolittle]. *Bid Me to Live: A Madrigal.* New York: Dial, 1960.

———. *Tribute to Freud.* New York: Pantheon, 1956.

———. *Trilogy.* 1944–46. New York: New Directions, 1998.

Herring, Philip. *Djuna: The Life and Work of Djuna Barnes.* New York: Viking, 1995.

Higonnet, Margaret R. "Not So Quiet in No-Woman's-Land." *Gendering War Talk.* Ed. Miriam Cooke and Angela Woollacott. Princeton: Princeton UP, 1993. 205–26.

Hogue, Cynthia. *Scheming Women: Poetry, Privilege, and the Politics of Subjectivity.* Albany: State U of New York P, 1995.

Holbrook, Susan. "Lifting Bellies, Filling Petunias, and Making Meanings through the Trans-Poetic." *American Literature* 71.4 (1999): 751–71.

Hollenberg, Donna Krolik, ed. *Between History and Poetry: The Letters of H.D. and Norman Holmes Pearson.* Iowa City: U of Iowa P, 1997.

———, ed. *H.D. and Poets After.* Iowa City: U of Iowa P, 2000.

Horvitz, Deborah M. *Literary Trauma: Sadism, Memory, and Sexual Violence in American Women's Fiction.* Albany: State U of New York P, 2000.

Kaplan, Ann E. *Trauma Culture: The Politics of Terror and Loss in Media and Literature.* New Brunswick: Rutgers UP, 2005.

LaCapra, Dominick. *Writing History, Writing Trauma.* Baltimore: Johns Hopkins UP, 2001.

Laity, Cassandra. *H.D. and the Victorian Fin de Siècle: Gender, Modernism, Decadence.* Cambridge: Cambridge UP, 1997.

Lesinska, Zofia. *Perspectives of Four Women Writers on the Second World War: Gertrude Stein, Janet Flanner, Kay Boyle, and Rebecca West.* Studies in Literary Criticism and Theory. New York: Peter Lang, 2002.

———. "Gertrude Stein's War Autobiographies: Reception, History, and Dialogue." *Literature, Interpretation, Theory* 9.4 (April 1999): 313–42.

Levenson, Michael H. *A Genealogy of Modernism: A Study of English Literary Doctrine, 1908–1922.* Cambridge: Cambridge UP, 1984.

Leys, Ruth. *Trauma: A Genealogy.* Chicago: U of Chicago P, 2000.

Lowell, Amy. *The Complete Poetical Works of Amy Lowell.* Boston: Houghton, 1955.

Lucas, Rose. "Re(reading)-Writing the Palimpsest of Myth." *Southern Review* 21.1 (1988): 43–57.

Malcolm, Janet. *Two Lives: Gertrude and Alice.* New Haven: Yale UP, 2007.

Marcus, Jane. "Laughing at Leviticus: *Nightwood* as Woman's Circus Epic." *Silence and Power: A Reevaluation of Djuna Barnes.* Ed. Mary Lynn Broe. Carbondale: Southern Illinois P, 1991. 221–50.

McCabe, Susan. *Cinematic Modernism: Modernist Poetry and Film.* Cambridge: Cambridge UP, 2005.

———. *Elizabeth Bishop: Her Poetics of Loss.* University Park: Pennsylvania State UP, 1994.

———. "'A Queer Lot' and the Lesbians of 1914: Amy Lowell, H.D., and Gertrude Stein." *Challenging Boundaries: Gender and Periodization.* Ed. Joyce W. Warren and Margaret Dickie. Athens: U of Georgia P, 2000. 62–92.

Mellow, James R. *Charmed Circle: Gertrude Stein and Company.* New York: Avon, 1974.

Miller, J. Hillis. "Narrative." *Critical Terms for Literary Study.* 2nd ed. Ed. Frank Lentricchia and Thomas McLaughlin. Chicago: U of Chicago P, 1995. 66–79.

Miller, Rosalind S. *Gertrude Stein: Form and Intelligibility.* New York: Exposition, 1949.

Mix, Deborah M. *A Vocabulary of Thinking: Gertrude Stein and Contemporary North American Women's Innovative Writing.* Iowa City: U of Iowa P, 2007.

Moi, Toril. *Sexual Textual Politics: Feminist Literary Theory.* London: Routledge, 1985.

Morris, Adalaide. *How to Live / What to Do: H.D.'s Cultural Poetics.* Urbana: U of Illinois P, 2003.

———. "Signaling: Feminism, Politics, and Mysticism in H.D.'s War *Trilogy.*" *Sagetrieb* 9.3 (1990): 121–33.

Nelson, Cary. "The Fate of Gender in Modern American Poetry." *Marketing Modernisms: Self-Promotion, Canonization, Rereading.* Ed. Kevin J. H. Dettmar and Stephen Watt. Ann Arbor: U of Michigan P, 1996. 321–60.

Neuman, Shirley, and Ira B. Nadel, eds. *Gertrude Stein and the Making of Literature.* Boston: Northeastern UP, 1988.

North, Michael. *Reading 1922: A Return to the Scene of the Modern.* New York: Oxford, 1999.

Olson, Liesl M. "Gertrude Stein, William James, and Habit in the Shadow of War." *Twentieth-Century Literature* 49.3 (Fall 2003): 328–59.

O'Neal, Hank. *"Life Is Painful, Nasty and Short . . . In My Case It Has Only Been Painful and Nasty": Djuna Barnes 1978–1981, An Informal Memoir.* New York: Paragon, 1990.

Owens, David M. "Gertrude Stein's 'Lifting Belly' and the Great War." *Modern Fiction Studies* 44.3 (1998): 608–18.

"Perverse." *The Oxford English Dictionary Online*, www.oed.com, 2007.

Plumb, Cheryl. Introduction. *Nightwood: The Original Version and Related Drafts*. By Djuna Barnes. Ed. Plumb. Normal, IL: Dalkey Archive, 1995. vii–xxvi.

———. "Revising *Nightwood*: 'a kind of glee of despair.'" *Review of Contemporary Literature* 13.3 (1993): 149–59.

Pound, Ezra. "A Few Don'ts by an Imagiste." 1913. *Manifesto: A Century of Isms*. Ed. Mary Ann Caws. Lincoln: U of Nebraska P, 2001. 356–59.

Reesman, Jeanne Campbell, ed. *Speaking the Other Self: American Women Writers*. Athens: U of Georgia P, 1997.

Rehling, Nicola. "Taking Patriarchy Out of Poetry: Eroticism and Subversion in Gertrude Stein's *Lifting Belly*." *Gramma: Journal of Theory and Criticism* 4 (1996): 77–87.

Rohman, Carrie. "Revising the Human: Silence, Being, and the Question of the Animal in *Nightwood*." *American Literature: A Journal of Literary History, Criticism, and Bibliography* 79.1 (2007): 57–84.

Sanyal, Debarati. *The Violence of Modernity: Baudelaire, Irony, and the Politics of Form*. Baltimore: Johns Hopkins UP, 2006.

Sbisà, Marina. "Subject and Gender in H.D.'s *Trilogy*." *H.D.'s Poetry: "the meanings that words hide*." Ed. Marina Camboni. New York: AMS, 2003. 91–113.

Scarry, Elaine. *The Body in Pain: The Making and Unmaking of the World*. New York: Oxford UP, 1985.

Scott, Bonnie Kime, ed. *Gender in Modernism: New Geographies, Complex Intersections*. Urbana: U of Illinois P, 2007.

———, ed. *The Gender of Modernism*. Bloomington: Indiana UP, 1990.

———. *Reconfiguring Modernism: The Women of 1928*. Vol. 1. Bloomington: Indiana UP, 1995.

Scott, James B. *Djuna Barnes*. Boston: Twayne, 1976.

Singer, Alan. *A Metaphorics of Fiction: Discontinuity and Discourse in the Modern Novel*. Tallahassee: UP of Florida, 1983.

Smith, Victoria L. "Generative Melancholy: Women's Loss and Literary Representation." *Mosaic: A Journal for the Interdisciplinary Study of Literature* 41.4 (2008): 95–110.

Stein, Gertrude. *Brewsie and Willie*. 1946. London: Brilliance, 1988.

———. *Lifting Belly*. 1953. Ed. Rebecca Mark. Tallahassee: Naiad, 1995.

———. *Mrs. Reynolds*. 1952. Los Angeles: Sun and Moon, 1995.

———. *Selected Writings of Gertrude Stein*. Ed. Carl Van Vechten. New York: Vintage, 1972.

———. *Wars I Have Seen*. 1945. London: Brilliance, 1984.

———. "The Winner Loses: A Picture of Occupied France." 1940. *Selected Writings of Gertrude Stein*. Ed. Carl Van Vechten. New York: Vintage, 1972. 615–37.

Steiner, Dorothea. "War and the Poem: Pattern and Ritual as (Anti)Strategies in Some Modernist Women Poets." *Red Badges of Courage: Wars and Conflicts in American Culture*. Ed. Biancamaria Pisapia, Rubeo Ugo, and Anna Scacchi. Proc. of the Associazione Italiana di Studi Nord-Americani XIII Biennial Conf., Oct. 25–27, 1995, U of Rome. Rome, Italy: Bulzoni Editore, 1998. 381–87.

Stewart, Victoria. "Introduction: Trauma and the Autobiographical." *Women's Autobiography: War and Trauma*. New York: Palgrave, 2003. 1–25.

Strozier, Charles B., and Michael Flynn, eds. *Trauma and Self*. Lanham, MD: Rowman and Littlefield, 1996.

Sword, Helen. *Engendering Inspiration: Visionary Strategies in Rilke, Lawrence, and H.D.* Ann Arbor: U of Michigan P, 1996.

Tal, Kalí. *Worlds of Hurt: Reading the Literature of Trauma*. Cambridge Studies in American Literature and Culture. New York: Cambridge UP, 1996.

Tate, Trudi. "H.D.'s War Neurotics." *Women's Fiction and the Great War*. Ed. Suzanne Raitt and Trudi Tate. Oxford: Clarendon, 1997. 241–62.

Taylor, Georgina. *H.D. and the Public Sphere of Modernist Women Writers, 1913–1946: Talking Women*. Oxford: Clarendon, 2001.

Thacker, Andrew. "Amy Lowell and H.D.: The Other Imagists." *Women : A Cultural Review* 4.1 (1993): 49–59.

Van der Kolk, Bessel A., Alexander C. McFarlane, and Lars Weisaeth, eds. *Traumatic Stress: The Effects of Overwhelming Experience on Mind, Body, and Society*. New York: Guilford, 1996.

Veltman, Laura J. "'The Bible Lies the One Way, but the Night-Gown the Other': Dr. Matthew O'Connor, Confession, and Gender in Djuna Barnes's *Nightwood*." *Modern Fiction Studies* 49.2 (2003): 204–27.

Wagner-Martin, Linda. *"Favored Strangers": Gertrude Stein and Her Family*. New Brunswick: Rutgers UP, 1995.

Warren, Joyce W., and Margaret Dickie, eds. *Challenging Boundaries: Gender and Periodization*. Athens: U of Georgia P, 2000.

Whitehead, Anne. *Trauma Fiction*. Edinburgh: Edinburgh UP, 2004.

Whittier-Ferguson, John. "The Liberation of Gertrude Stein: War and Writing." *Modernism/modernity* 8.3 (2001): 405–28.

———. "Stein in Time: History, Manuscripts, Memory." *Modernism/modernity* 6.1 (1999): 115–51.

Will, Barbara. "Gertrude Stein, Bernard Fäy, and the Ruthless Flowers of Friendship." *Modernism/modernity* 15.4 (2008): 647–63.

Willis, Elizabeth. "A Public History of the Dividing Line: H.D., the Bomb, and the Roots of the Postmodern." *Arizona Quarterly: A Journal of American Literature, Culture, and Theory* 63.1 (2007): 81–108.

Woolf, Virginia. *A Room of One's Own.* 1929. New York: Fall River, 2007.

Zajdel, Melody M. "'I See Her Differently': H.D.'s *Trilogy* as Feminist Response to Masculine Modernism." *Sagetrieb* 5.1 (1986): 7–15.

— Index —